Giordana

ALCOHOLISM AND STIGMA

A Family involved in the Joust of Alcoholism
While fighting to Build
Al-Anon in Italy

Youcanprint

Title | Alcoholism and Stigma.
The Story of two Lives who Fight to build Al-Anon in Italy
Author | Giordana
ISBN | 978-88-31648-37-0

Giordana's Channel | *FORYOU TUBENEWS*

Youcanprint
Via Marco Biagi 6 - 73100 Lecce
www.youcanprint.it
info@youcanprint.it

Based on a true story. For reasons of privacy, the names have been changed. The contents and ideas expressed in this book are to be considered the author's personal opinion and experiences; and therefore does not bind the publisher in any way.

The images included in the text are exclusively for illustrative and explanatory purposes. The author does not intend to use them to harm the rights of others. They are old photos, and some are of low quality, but constitute a relevant historical testimony. They are private property.

What thou lovest well remains,
the rest is dross
What thou lov'st well shall not be reft from thee
What thou lov'st well is thy true heritage

Ezra Pound (Canto LXXXI)

I dedicate these memories

To my twin brother Mario

To my parents
For having led their life in such a way that
their children today can be proud of it

To Maria
For her unique moral and intellectual qualities
and for being an irreplaceable friend
without which this book wouldn't have taken shape
nor would it ever have been completed

To Hernany
For her collaboration

To Damian Tharcisius,
who reviewed and edited
the English edition more than once,
with great dedication and beyond expectations!

*In the story, two lives wind along
a dramatic thread, in the fight against alcoholism within the family
and the difficulties they face in a non-profit organization, from the
time of its founding.*

Introductory Note

It's the 90's. Leonella and Laura, for the first time, interweave their experiences involving an association that supports the relatives of people suffering from alcoholism, and their own lives. This 'story' links the problem of addiction at home (via *Fragments*), to the issues of the Association (the newly emerging Association of Family and Friends of Alcoholics Anonymous – Al-Anon).

The reconstruction of the memories, which emerged intermittently over the period of forty years, finally came to an end on November 2018.

The narrative voice is that of Laura[1].

Leonella's paragraphs are written in italics and bear her signature (L. died in 2014).

In support of the facts narrated, an extract of the documents belonging to the private paper archive of the protagonists, are cited in the Appendix.

Leonella and Laura, during the interviews, often reiterated that the negative events were due to the actions of individuals and not to Al-Anon as an association. In all our conversations, they continued to refer to the non-profit and its efforts, as a gift from God to all those who have an alcoholic family member or friend. For this reason, they spared no effort in contributing to the birth of Al-Anon in Italy. Even to the point of enduring stigma. They fought for Al-Anon to become an instrument of healing and unity in Italy: a rescue vessel, into which those in need could find refuge from the sea of despair. Al-Anon: which today has become a crystalline Association, that is renowned across the world for its efforts. This tale, marks the Italian version of its origins.

---

[1] Laura is the daughter of Leonella.

To better understand the Text

Imagine a Theatre with three alternate stages

First Stage – *The Story of Al-Anon*

We have two narrative voices, or 'actors': Laura and Leonella.
The Paragraphs written by Leonella are preceded by her name.
Laura and Leonella speak about their problems involving the Association from its beginning. As they worked inside Al-Anon as volunteers from the very start.

Inside the Association they had different tasks: Leonella was translating, whilst Laura was volunteering inside the Group. For this reason they sometimes experience the same events together. At other times, each of them present their own version of the journey, and together they reconstruct the story.

Second stage - *Fragments (the contemporary life of the protagonists, at their home)*

The narrative voice is only of Laura. Leonella died in 2014. Laura wrote *Fragments* only recently.

Laura wants the reader-living *on the other side*-seeing the problems that she and her mother experience at home. The *Fragments* are intended to allow the reader to become acquainted with the personages, and to be aware, that behind the story of the Association there are human beings with their deeply personal dramas.

Laura expresses her views via flashbacks. Each one of them is isolated. They follow the order of time.

Third Stage - *Mario's dramas*

Laura wants the reader *seeing* the tragedy that Mario is living through.

She attempts this by shedding light on his life: capturing the most tragic moments. For this reason the *title* of the concerned paragraphs are all written on the right hand, and are presented on purpose at the end of the Al-Anon Chapters: Chapters 1-3-5-7. Chapter 9 is dedicated solely to Mario.

***

Laura never allows the reader to forget Mario. He is always *there;* when Laura lights the *Third Stage* with flashbacks, at the end of the Chapters dedicated to the Association; or because Laura speaks about him in the *Fragments.* Or when the entire Chapter is dedicated to him.

1949 – Far from problems.
From left to right: Laura, Leonella, Alessandro, Mario.

To all the Al-Anon [2].
To all those who will never stop fighting
for the defense of human dignity.

My name is Laura, and I am an Al-Anon.

Since *Truth* is one of the fundamental values of every life and social structure, I have decided to share my story and my experiences involving all the Al-Anon members. In so doing, I also share them with anyone who wants to benefit of them. Confronting the truth about ourselves and others is the basis of the Recovery Program proposed by both Al-Anon and Alcoholics Anonymous (A.A.). Facing social difficulties from various types of people encountered in Al-Anon, is an experience that is characteristic of most social groups of any time. This commonality of experience is what makes Al-Anon valid on a global level.

It is meaningful the path that the Association had set up in Italy. For if you remain firm in the vision outlined by the Steps, the Traditions and the Service Concepts that are the basis of Al-Anon for the individual recovery, difficulties shall smooth out.

It is a fair estimate, that to date, Al-Anon has helped or saved the lives of millions of people, who were once caught in the joust of alcoholism.

---

[2] In the text, both the *Association of A.A.* and the *A.A.'s Members* are sometimes shortly called *A.A.* The same goes for *Al-Anon.*

Il Messaggero

9 novembre 1972

Thanks to Santino of 'Al-Anon/Udine 1'
For putting the article at our disposal.

*For the sake of fluency, we have chosen not to
repeat 'he or her' every time.
Therefore
the masculine form is also meant to include the feminine one.*

Chapter One

A carefully guarded phone number

> *Dad is not there. He must work.*
> *Alessandro is not there. I do not know where he is.*

Leonella - First contact with A.A.: a person with a kind voice answers the phone.

I can't talk about the beginning of Al-Anon in Italy without talking about A.A.

On 6 May 1972, an alcoholic named Carlo goes to the American Group of A.A. in Via Napoli 58 seeking help; a place already frequented by some other Italian alcoholics.

Carlo is the first alcoholic to achieve sobriety, and so strives to help others achieve the same result.

Carlo, in October 1972, lays the foundations for the first Italian-speaking Group of A.A., in Via Napoli. Later on, he also has an article published on the same subject, in a national newspaper.

'Il Messaggero', on 9 November 1972, published the news of the existence of an A.A. Group: which helps people having trouble with alcohol to find release. Also included is a phone number for those seeking more information. The article is by Sandro Cova.

I read the article and kept the newspaper, although I am not sure if the incomprehensible behavior of my son Mario, is due to the abuse of alcoholic beverages.

On October 1973, following my son's request, I dial the number that I had carefully guarded until then.

A kind voice answers. We make an appointment to go and see Mario at his house. At the door, waiting for me is a tall, charming guy, with long white hair. His name is Pietro. We enter Mario's home together, and the first contact, both for my son and myself, is made.
Pietro (1973).

The day when my desperate Mother pulls out of a drawer that jealously guarded piece of paper, I am with her.

My Mother explains to the person who answers the phone, what the problem is: her son Mario has been drinking for years. He is ruining his life and has made our family life unmanageable; what is worse is that nobody can help him or give relief to his suffering.

The answer, comes in the form a man named Pietro. Without wasting any time, he gives us some information that rained down on our minds like water on a barren land: giving us a new lease of life.

The first point: family members are not responsible for the alcoholism of the compulsive drinker.

The second point: A.A. only helps alcoholics who are willing to change, and are clearly seeking help for this reason. So far everything is alright, because Mario whilst desperate, was also willing.

But what left us speechless is the third point he makes.

When my Mother asks: *"Well, then of course, for the reimbursement of expenses or if there are costs.."*

Pietro interrupts her: *"Madam, we do what we do for ourselves. And there will never be anything to be paid."*

Later, Mama will tell me: *"Laura, we met angels. It's incredible. They don't even want the gasoline reimbursement."*

For people who can't even imagine what chronic stress is like: one which lasts one, two, three, even ten or twenty years... During which time you have spent large amounts of money, suffered every anxiety and delusion. Hence I think it is difficult to understand the range of feelings that such words can produce: amazement, disbelief, wonder, suspicion (will it be true?), and fear of another disappointment.

A few days later, going to the appointment, we realize that *yes,* angels do exist. They are the *recovered Alcoholics* who help other people like them to get out of the alcohol addiction.

They are known, all over the world, as *Alcoholics Anonymous.*

The appointment for the first contact is with Pietro, in via dei Banchi Nuovi, at Mario's home.

Pietro was a man with simple manners who possessed an unconscious charisma. Mario loved intelligent people with simple social backgrounds. He related to them without anxiety and with great affection.

The contact with Pietro left a deep impression on him.

Pietro was tall and thin. His face seemed to be carved of wood. He was about sixty years old, and made no secret of having been imprisoned for a certain period of time. Although we never knew why. In relationships, he was immediate, communicative and direct.

Mario was impressed. He started attending A.A., and my Mother and I, Al-Anon.

At the time, as already mentioned, *there was another A.A. personage, whose name was 'Carlo'.*

However, Mario tied himself to Pietro.

Notes on A.A.

Attendance in A.A., is not mandatory. They slowly set the person concerned upon the path of spiritual recovery, through *The Twelve Steps* (see Appendix). The journey ends with the *Twelfth Step*, which consists in *bringing to others the message that recovery is possible.*

It is a journey that lasts a lifetime because alcoholism is a disease from which one never heals. A bit like diabetes: it is possible to neutralize its effects, but you remain diabetic.

The *active alcoholic* neutralizes the effects of his illness by agreeing not to be able to control his alcohol intake and giving up drinking, thus becoming a *sober alcoholic*. Should he touch the alcohol again, he will go back to square one. The relapses will always be worse and can lead to death. The mechanism is the same for all addictions.

I have witnessed, albeit indirectly, several *relapses* and can testify to the validity of these statements.

All that has been said so far about the A.A. is mostly valid also for Al-Anon.

Inside A.A. and Al-Anon, *anonymity* is secured: no one knows the surname of anyone else.

Alcoholics, as well as their families and friends, attend *closed meetings*, to which no outsider is allowed. As well as *open meetings*, in which A.A. and Al-Anon meet together.

Occasionally they invite professionals, such as doctors, lawyers, judges, who might be interested in the topic of alcohol recovery. These forums are referred to as *open meeting* dedicated to *public information.*

In this particular case, the whole Group is warned well in advance, so that those who do not wish to be seen, can avoid going.

During the fifteen years in which I have been able to observe these two associations, from within, I realized that A.A., compared to other groups which deal with alcoholism, to its credit, has the most number of successes.

The other private or regional institutions, that deal with alcohol, although widely borrowing the guide-lines from A.A.-and therefore are based on A.A.'s principles- never fully respect its spirit. For this reason the desired results may not follow. Some require fees for entry. Others act through coercive or humiliating mechanisms, and in almost all of them, there are external interference: in the form of professional classes, whose self-serving logic, is invariably linked to the acquisition of customers. Whilst some other structures accept funds allocated by the Regions for drug addiction recovery.

When entering A.A. or Al-Anon, no general or sensitive data is needed. Just the name. There are no obligations to attend meetings, nor are there are any fees to be paid. Every evening the members *pass the hat*, and those who can give, give what they can. Neither psychologists, nor psychiatrists, nor doctors, nor priests are present in their professional capacity.

A.A. and Al-Anon, by statute, cannot accept funding from anyone for any reason. This is why, over time, both associations succeeded in remaining independent from any political and/or religious influences.

A.A. is an association established in America in 1935. The purpose of A.A. is to help people to recover from alcoholism.

Lois throws a shoe at her sober husband... and Al-Anon is born.

Sixteen years after the birth of A.A., Lois–the wife of one of the A.A.'s founders-after a furious quarrel with her longstanding, but sober husband, hurled at him one of her shoes. Thus she realizes that the recovery of her alcoholic husband, has not restored her peace. She concludes that family members also need help, which they can give to each other by sharing their experiences.

As a consequence, in 1951 a new association is born. It is Al-Anon (Families and Friends of Alcoholics Anonymous). It acts in support of people whose life has been upset by their relationships with alcoholics.

From the outset, the acronym Al-Anon was used as a noun to define the association, and as an adjective to refer to its members.

After an empty gap of thirty-seven years, the first A.A. Group arises in 1972 in Italy.

The first Al-Anon Group will arise almost simultaneously, but its path will be fraught with many difficulties.

In 1990 a handful of Al-Anon reconstruct the first ten, difficult years of Al-Anon in Italy, from 1974 to 1983. This was the team: Leonella, Enrica, Maria Grazia, Mara of A.A. and myself.

The example set by the pioneers who fought to defend the integrity of Al-Anon using the Steps, Traditions, and Service Concepts as effective tools, emerges from our stories.

Pietro dies, sober. Giancarla and Elisa commit suicide.

In A.A., Mario is tied very much to Giancarla, a former manne-
quin. Beautiful, funny, sophisticated, forty, and hopelessly alcoholic.
After a few months that Mario attended the Group, Giancarla
killed herself. My brother went to her funeral.

Giancarla's legs had been badly folded to close the lid of the coffin, which was too small. Mario got completely upset and furious.
Not long afterward-perhaps one year later-Pietro also died, sober.
Mario could not withstand this second blow. He started drinking
again and stopped going to the Group. He takes the road of A.A.
several times, but combined with his chemical addiction, he never
fully escapes this desperate situation.

Fifteen years after these facts, Mario was again tied to an alcoholic
and drug-addicted young woman: Elisa at the time was about twen-
ty-five years old. She had an uncommon intelligence and was tormented and restless, continually escaping from an authoritarian father and from a mother deeply, who was tied to social conventions.
Elisa counted an abortion among her traumas. The family con-
demned her for being pregnant and, in fact, this was one of the elements that led her to get rid of her child.
On the day of admission to the hospital, her parents denied her the
comfort of their presence: they didn't want neither a "bastard" nor an
abortion. I know this story because she asked me to accompany her.
Which I did.
Not long after, Elisa took her own life. Before committing suicide,
she looked for my brother several times, but was unable to contact
him.

A beautiful afternoon in May (1974).

It's a beautiful May afternoon, and I go down via Nazionale in
Roma, the city where I was born and have always lived. I come

from the University, after having just failed the test of my first and last set of exams at the Economics and Business Faculty La Sapienza. I had attacked the math exam, the most difficult one, without covering the bases.

'Well- I think as I look at the windows -I will study this Summer, and I will give the exam back in September.'

Stirring with these thoughts, I approach the Church of Via Napoli[3] walking idly. The Church since 1972, on certain days and hours, welcomes the Alcoholics Anonymous: those who had the opportunity to give life to the first A.A. Group in Italy[4]

Subsequently, a second room had been made available to Al-Anon. To the people whose life is linked to the trials of alcoholism. It's almost six o'clock in the afternoon: Time for a meeting, according to the Al-Anon Group timetable. My Mother, since the year before[5], often goes to the Via Napoli. Thus I know that this afternoon she would be there. So I think: *'I should jump in and go home with her.'* At the time we lived in the Eur District, ten kilometers from the very center of Roma, where Via Napoli is situated.

I enter Via Napoli 58 and, in a small room at the end of a corridor, I find Mamma and other people sitting on the seats of the kindergarten children. Evidently, there is a day of the week, in which the Church hosts kindergarten children.

I am thin and small, yet I struggle to find a comfortable position on the small chair.

---

[3] Church of Saint Paul's within the Walls.

[4] Later it was discovered that, at the same time, other groups were rising in Italy.

[5] 1973.

Wendi

A young woman is speaking; her name is Wendy. She is an alcoholic and also an Al-Anon.

It was the first testimony I heard directly from the voice of an alcoholic, and it hit me hard.

"My name is Wendy, and I am alcohol-addicted. Having in my turn an alcoholic husband, I am also a family member of an alcoholic. therefore, I am also an Al-Anon."

Meanwhile, we observe the most absolute silence. For in both Associations[6], we allow one person to speak at a time, and no one ever interrupts those who are giving their testimony. In this way, discussions never arise. Everyone talks about his/her own life and experiences. Those who find the testimonies useful, they take it; otherwise, they simply choose to ignore it.

Wendy goes on: *"When I noticed my husband's alcoholism, I tried to do something, but everything was useless. I came home tired at night, and could not talk to him. We always fought. I started suffering from horrible headaches, and no way I could overcome them. One evening, by chance, I took a sip of whiskey. The headache ended immediately.*

Great. At least something was going well. That was how I became alcohol addicted: one sip at a time, one evening after another. Until I realized that I also had become an alcoholic like my husband. Without being aware of it. Unintentionally. Dragging me into this disease was the effect that alcohol produced in my body and in my mind. The relief it gave me."

---

[6] A.A. and Al-Anon.

AA. was born in the United States. Wendy, being an American, an alcoholic, and the wife of an alcoholic, had no trouble reading the official literature in English.

Being well informed about the mechanics of the Groups, she was very helpful for both the alcoholics and the family members.

Alcoholism is a Disease

My Mother and I attend the Group because for over twenty years, our lives have been linked to the problems of alcoholism.

Mario started drinking at twelve (1954), albeit in minimal doses. When we meet A.A., in 1972, Mom and I have already spent eighteen years dealing with anxieties and behaviors that are partly negligible and partly harmful, both for him and for us.

Now we know that alcoholism-as the World Health Organization affirms-is a disease, and that relatives and friends are not to be blamed for.

For the alcoholic patient, we can do little. In fact, we can only do one thing: we can help him to become *aware* that his problem is the alcohol. This means to stop trying to protect him, follow him, control him, and above all, stop trying to help him with suggestions that may seem good to us, but is never good enough for him.

We must accept -and this is the really hard part- that the alcoholic has the right to his pain, and that he is the only one who has the power to change his life.

People who die due to alcohol related abuses, are more than you know. The reason is that many deaths caused by alcohol are classified in other ways: heart attack, car accident, murder, suicide, liver cirrhosis etc.

Where does this accursed illness come from? The origins can be different, and sometimes there are multiple causes. To get out of it, however, it is not necessary to establish *where does it come out*: it is only required *to stop drinking*. Because the disease of alcoholism can be contained, like diabetes; but not entirely cured.

The alcoholic who rebels, and tries to control his addiction, is going to meet *a relapse* from which he would struggle to recover.

If we really want to investigate the causes, we can say that one of them is *heredity*. We inherit the genes of someone in our family who was an alcoholic, one or more generations before.

Unfortunately, for Mario, the situation is doubly dangerous, as Mario is an alcoholic but also reliant on drugs.

That evening, when I went to Via Napoli to fetch my Mother, I didn't know that I would stay in Al-Anon, in service for another fifteen years; and that in doing so, I would give up attending University.

I'm thirty-three years old and I have been working in the Bank since I was seventeen. When I get out of the Office, it is already six o'clock in the evening. The little time available in the evening is not enough to take courses at the University and also to volunteer. I have to make a choice. One of the two roads must be abandoned.

Going to University had been one of the most important aims of my life. However the private high school I had attended did not allow me to do it directly. So for two whole years-whilst working-I made the sacrifice to get an accounting diploma recognized by the state: two years without ever watching television or going out! Because Saturdays, Sundays, and holidays were reserved for my personal study. In the end, I graduated with top marks. And now, having at last the possibility to attend the University, after so many sacrifices, I was at a crossroad. I thought about it for almost a month. Then, following my social vocation, I choose Al-Anon.

Leonella – "When translating, it seems to me I'm speaking to my son."

Not long after my first contact with A.A., an alcoholic tells me that, on Saturdays, I too can attend their Group, because the meeting is 'open', which means that family members can also participate.

So I begin to frequent them, to hear testimonies, and to understand more things about their efforts.

I soon learn that for A.A., there is specialized Literature, but very little has been translated. There are only a few typed photocopies, all in a poor state.

Translating had always fascinated me, and for several years I was working for some movie houses. So I immediately offer my time to translate something. Further, to acquire the right terminology, I will continue to attend the open meetings.

Moreover, when translating, it seems to me I'm speaking to my son. For my hope is that one day he will be able to read these papers, attend, understand, become sober.

Nobody at the time was thinking about making publications or printing in typography. Where could we find the money to pay for such things? We had to contend ourselves with translating and photocopying. So it will be in A.A., as it was in Al-Anon. But the result was disastrous, because the photocopies quickly get ruined.

Just in the same period they tell me that, abroad there are Groups for family members and friends of alcoholics, and that I can contact an Al-Anon member of the English Group, to open an Italian one. However, I dedicate myself entirely to the task of translating for A.A. Since, I do not understand what the 'Groups for relatives' could be useful for. So I continue to go to Via Napoli to bring the translations that are only acceptable to the alcoholics. Which they welcome with great enthusiasm. As for the publications, it will only be in 1977, that A.A. will constitute its first Service Committee, and that I will be appointed Coordinator for 'their' Literature.

Leonella – An embittered Wendi goes back to America: Abi wanted to kick her out the Group.

Towards the end of 1974, as usual I went to A.A. to bring the translation. Once again the alcoholics urge me to attend the meetings of Al-Anon held by Wendy, which is already followed by Laura.

In the very first period, before Wendy started holding meetings, the following question emerged: What about the plight of 'alcoholic family members' who accompany the alcoholics, and wait behind the closed door? The door behind which a 'closed-meeting' is taking place?

Well, to spend the time they talk to each other about this and that, often forced to stand up owing to the lack seating; and when they can find chairs and a table, they 'play cards'.

Laura has already mentioned why the initiative to open an Al-Anon Group was taken by an alcoholic, but I would like to go back to it. Wendy is both an alcoholic and the wife of an alcoholic, which often puts her in crisis. So without appropriate help, she is afraid of falling back into alcohol use. She needs to see the problem 'from the other side'. She needs support not only as an alcoholic, but also as a 'family member of an alcoholic'. Thus, with the encouragement of A.A., who had unsuccessfully turned to me, she had opened the first Al-Anon Italian Group.

Wendy, on one evening, when rummaging through an old Church closet full of papers, finds some pamphlets destined for Al-Anon, and immediately gives them to me, for translation.

Reading the 'Al-Anon Literature' I understand, without any further doubt, the importance of organizing groups for the relatives of the alcoholic.

Hence I begin to translate also for Al-Anon without ceasing to work for A.A.

Wendy teaches us the importance of following the Program, and of marking knowledgeable to everyone, at any time: both the presence of, and the 'amount of collected money'.

However, later, without informing me, she contacts the 'Al-Anon WSO' in New York. She sends them copies of my first translations and asks for the 'copyrights'. In this case, 'copyright' means both the approval of the translation and the permission to reproduce their texts.

She also mentions me as a contact. The reason is, at that moment, I am the only person who knows English and can translate, and hence be able to manage a correspondence.

The 'copyrights' arrive punctually from America: not even one correction was ever requested.

You don't have to be surprised if I speak of 'corrections'. It is not always easy to make sense of what is being said in a foreign language, when translating it into your own language; at the same time maintaining the meaning of the original text.

In 1977, when Wendy goes back to America, she leaves a lot of gratitude in her wake: for the work she had done with Al-Anon in Italy, but also a feeling of hostility with a certain 'Abi'. Abi (fancy name) [7]. A person who made her life very difficult within the Group. Abi held that an alcoholic could not attend an Al-Anon Group. So, according to her, Wendy 'had to be thrown out!'

Mario - Vicolo del Trifone

It's two o'clock in the morning when we are woken up by the ringing phone. It is always night when alarming phone calls arrive at our home.

---

[7] With this position, Abi - one of the first Al-Anon   members - makes her entrance as a "protagonist" in these events. Abi considers as a personal enemy anyone she believes she cannot control.

This time it is Mauro Bronchi de *Le Sorelle Bandiera*[8]. Perhaps someone still remembers him. Poor boy: how many hopes, how many disappointments. Mauro is one of the few friends left close to Mario.

There is no time even to think. In one second, Mom and I are downstairs, and we jump on her Bianchina, a very small car.

Between him and us there are ten endless miles of traffic lights and intersections, only partially turned off.

I drive. It's like being in a dark corridor at the end of which you don't know what kind of pain you're going to fall into, and you throw yourself against it to get it over as soon as possible.

I devour the road with my eyes before the wheels bite it. I stare at the asphalt: as if in so doing, I could gut time's wall that separates us from *our* alcoholic.

Finally, we arrive, get out of the car, rush up the stairs and ring the bell. It is not one of Mario's worst suicide attempts. He is lying in the bed, but he has recovered. He has swallowed too many pills, but this time, he will make it. A hospitalization seems useless. Mauro stays by his side until morning. After that night, he too will disappear from his life.

---

[8] The *Flag Sisters* were a comical and a musical trio active between 1976 and 1992, originally launched as part of the television program *L'altra domenica*, conducted by Renzo Arbore.

Chapter Two

Fragments
Alcoholism
A wind blowing from far away

> *Dad is not there. He must work.*
> *Alessandro is not there. I do not know where he is.*

Grandfather Francesco.

In my family, there has been an alcoholic: grandfather Francesco. My Mother's father, born in Senigallia.

I don't know how my maternal grandparents met, but I know they were broke. All their life, they fought to pay the bills at the end of the month.

My grandparents lived their lives thanks to a stand selling household items in Piazza dei Macelli, in front of the Foro Annonario, the ancient fish-market of Senigallia, which is still the center of the town. The *Bar della Vanda*, the only one at the time that could boast a billiard-room, has now another name. Unfortunately, the billiard-room was dismantled to make room for the tables, but the bar still looks over the square.

Francesco and Gina had only one daughter: Leonella, who married Ernesto, and in turn had three children: Alessandro, the eldest son, and afterward, the twins: Mario and Laura.

At the time of our childhood, we used to spend our summer holidays in our grandparents' house. I remember the neglected draft land behind the house, where Mario and I played with the ducks. We chased them, to catch and put cute, colorful ribbons around their necks. Then we tried to make them swim in a tub, no more than a meter wide. The luckless ducks rushed away, terrified as they were chased by us. We were happy.

The house was really humble. The bricks of the floor hadn't been leveled for a very long time. Drinking water was fetched from the *Fontana dell' Oca* (Goose Fountain). The bathroom consisted of a small room with a cup, and we washed in a tub located inside the large room in front of it, with water heated over the fire.

During the summer, I couldn't wait to go there.

I remember the sound of the rope-maker and the extended row of easels, placed along the road leading to the sea-side. The taste of the fruit bought along the street. But above all, I remember my grandparents' stall and its thousands of items.

I was fascinated by the glass-made ears of wheat, the Ginori's ceramics, but also by the stainless steel pots. I could not know what 'stainless steel' was, but from the tone my grandmother used when speaking to the customers, I understood that it had to be something extraordinary. The flashes of metal confirmed my theory.

It was nice to help my grandparents in the square. It was also lovely, at mid-morning to eat *Mancinelli's pizza*. Mancinelli, the best baker and rotisserie of Senigallia, situated at the time -and remains to this date- next to the Vanda bar. The stall was just ten meters from our favorite eating-point.

At one o'clock my grandparents dismantled everything and made preparations for opening it the next day. When this process started, I was thrilled to help. I was having fun. The stall emptied, and the cart which was supposed to carry everything to the store was filled up. Then Grandpa lifted it by the handles and allowed me to place a hand next to his. Pushing it slowly, we climbed up behind the Duomo in via Carlo Pisacane, and then made our way to the depository. Once there, the cart had to be emptied, and everything was put back on the shelves.

The next morning, at dawn, my grandparents started everything again. I never understood why they didn't leave everything on the cart, instead of restocking it the following day. There must have been a reason, but I still do not know what it was.

At the end of the 1940s, although broke, the standard of living of my grandparents had improved.

Gina and Francesco, newlyweds in the early 1900s, lived in rent and in addition to the cart, they owned a horse. *His* name was Grillo (Cricket), and at the time he was still a lean and agile horse. Grillo had probably known better times. Perhaps this was why he was restless, and often kicked nervously around with his hind legs.

Mama told me more than once how, one day when she entered the stable and threw herself on one of Grillo's hind legs to embrace him, the horse, instead of kicking as usual, remained motionless: Grillo had realized that a child had thrown itself on his hocks. After so many years, Mom was still speaking of Grillo with deep love.

In that first period, while my grandmother devoted herself to the *square* in Senigallia; at two o'clock in the morning my grandfather, in the summer and winter, was already running with Grillo, up and down the hills of the Marchigiano.

The wobbly lantern was the only light then. They ran to be ready at seven in the morning, in order to not miss the passage of the first housewives. They *ran* to be on time at the fairs of the various countries. And on cold winter nights, grandfather carried the wine flask with him. Drinking was the way for penniless people to keep a bit warm.

It was the year 1910. At the time, no one knew that, in reality, this mechanism (of drinking as a remedy) is perverse. The warmth it generated was deceptive, and the more you drink, the colder you ultimately became. And the Alcoholics Anonymous was years away.

I imagine that, over time, grandfather Francesco started drinking even if it wasn't cold.

Drinking was also a way to socialize and to exchange a few words with someone, late in the afternoon after work ended. Not knowing what else to do, he started to go to the tavern.

He was such a simple and solitary man that even the Vanda billiard-room was closed to him.

I still hear Mom's voice: *"Hey, kids! go and call your grandfather."* Which also was a game for us.

We ran down the stairs, we crossed Via del Barroccio, and went through a narrow alley -which even today, does not have a name- and from there, we turned immediately to the right, and entered the *Osteria di Gigi.* Grandpa was there. *"Grandpa, it's dinner time!"* Grandpa got up and came. When we grew up, Mom, told us that most of the time he was a little drunk.

From that time, I myself inherited a sugar problem: I can only drink if I put sugary substances in the water. Although fortunately, for some time now, I have become accustomed to replacing the urge for something sweet with something bitter... sometimes.

Which is significant, if we consider that in the first phase of detoxification, alcoholics drink sugary substances to alleviate the symptoms of abstinence and the desire for alcohol.

Alessandro, between thirty-five and forty, stopped drinking.

Mario instead was consumed by his addictions.

Alessandro: an obedient child

There was one person who knew the reason for the perennial quarrels between Alessandro and Mario: disputes that in adulthood resulted in a dramatic break. That person was my Mother, and she repeated that story to me many times.

Alessandro is two and a half years old, and is an adorable child: cute, polite and obedient. The time comes when Mom has to leave him for a few days to go to the hospital to give birth to the twins: Mario and I. She leaves him alone at home with her Mother: for us, grandmother Gina:

"Mom, please. When I return, I will not be able to embrace Alexander because I will have the twins in my arms."

At the time, The Second World War was just ended. From recollection, two things appear evident: Dad, was often absent for some reason (at the time he was a lieutenant in the Army), and Mamma wanted to avoid a traumatic meeting of the firstborn with the newborns. *"Mom, please, when I come back from the hospital, keep Alessandro away from the entrance. Let him play until I can hug him and explain him that he now has a little brother and a little sister"*.

On the big day Leonella rings the door bell, grandmother Gina goes to open, and Mom, entering sees what she most feared: Alessandro is sitting just in the entrance, on a chair.

In the days when Leonella was absent, Alessandro has had a bad stomach ache, and he is now anxiously waiting to be re-embraced by her.

When Alessandro sees her, he pales: his Mom, in her arms, has two strange mewing *bundles*. Mom can do nothing other than hurry to past him, and go to put her bundles somewhere.

Then she runs back to Alessandro, to his beloved child. But it is too late. An irreversible damage has been done to his fragile psyche.

From that day onwards, Alessandro appears displeased and rebellious. He no longer obeys, adopts a defiant tones, stops using cutlery, and throws everything on the ground. It is his way of protesting the suffering caused by the presence of the twins.

According to the stories of our Mother, the relationship between Alessandro and us, the twins, was irreparably compromised on that day.

As events would prove, Alessandro, at twenty-two, will break his ties with Mario and, according to my understanding, he will never show any sign of acknowledging the presence of a sister at home. The pain my Mother has been carrying with her all her life, because of that episode, was intense. Considering the number of times she will talk about it with me during her life.

After a number of years, involving home-changes, deaths, births, quarrels and joys, there came a moment when, opening by chance, a drawer in Mom's bedroom, I found a very special picture of Alexander. The photo of a nice little child, taken before the twins were born. When he still was *her* Alexander.

In Italy, they consider the psychologist as a misfortune, reserved to madmen and eccentrics.

After the war, my Father –who had graduated in Economics and Commerce, learnt to do what it takes to provide for his wife and three children. First he was an agent for a firm producing ceramics in Faenza; afterwards, he became an agent for an English scarf producing firm.

I still have in my closet a scarf of that time. It reminds me of the evening when, curious, we crowded around him, and he showed us the sample-book: colors, colors, and colors.

I still have the ink-holder of Faenza, in which I have so many times seen him dipping his pen with the nib.

Dad wanted to teach mathematics at the University, but the assistants, even at the time, were not paid.

Around this time, he often, for periods of time, stay away from home. This is after he agrees to become a representative for the 'olives processing machines' for the area of Southern Italy. At a time when the highways were still have to come and transportation was slow.

Usually, he stays away for a fortnight, and when he comes back home; in order to produce a serene atmosphere, Mamma does not tell him about the problems that three children cause.

Alessandro was born on 15 July 1940.

I was born in 1942, half an hour before midnight; Mario half an hour later. I always thought that life separated us just in that moment. Mario and I are heterozygous twins: I don't have what he has and vice versa. He is cute, cheerful, funny. He seems to be able to do everything with an artistic sense: he can sing, dance, draw; everyone is attracted to him.

When someone makes a compliment, they give it to Mario. And if someone asks Mom to take one of the twins home for one night, they ask to host Mario.

I witness all this as if I were watching a movie; I simply take it as a natural fact whose mechanisms are unknown to me.

On the other hand, *Mariolino* seems haunted by an adverse fate: he has many beautiful qualities, but also an overly nervous and sensitive character. Which prevents him from making use of his talents.

We are seven or eight years old and when-albeit rarely-guests arrive at our home. At which point Mario cries desperately at the idea of having to go out and say *good morning*.

It is 1957. Mario and I are fifteen years old. It was a time when consulting a psychologist is seen as a mockery reserved for madmen and eccentrics. If it hadn't been so, I believe that my Mother would have sought support for herself and for Mario.

Nor were there, at the time any sports or social centers for children.   Not that it would have mattered. Since our family couldn't have afforded the extra expenses.

Nothing is lacking at home. But that is only because my Mother asks for '*120 grams of meat, please!*' And when Umberto, the butcher announces '*125 Madam. Is it okay?*' She replies '*No, thanks. I want five less.*' She is meticulous with the finances. For if she didn't act in such a way, at the end of the month, the table would have been empty.

Dad and Mom both were born in needy families and grew up in humble environments. But they were endowed with extraordinary intelligence. Hence both succeeded in working and paying for their own studies.

Mario, brilliant and multifaceted, looked like my Mother.

Mom knows how to make or turn clothes with the same skill with which she runs a pension, translates films from English for the renowned studios: Metro Goldwin Meyer and the Warner Brothers. Or how she organizes the Church's welfare activities. The same skill she puts into her medicine studies. She, who seemed destined to work in the square behind the counter, shall go onto win a scholarship and shall become a Red Cross Nurse and Assistant in the surgical room, next to Prof. Paride Stefanini.

Mario, over time, asserts his individuality and his destiny in a thousand ways. He loves to dress the two small statuettes located in our sitting room, and this infuriates my Father who forbids him from doing it (later, he will become a set and costume designer).

He is twelve when the first nightmares begin. We are in Senigallia, at the time when Mamma runs a small pension (1952-1954). Mario, in the afternoon, drinks alcoholic aperitifs taken from the bar, without realizing the risks he is running: it's a game for him, but it also the beginning of a carousel with a painful culmination. Mario finishes middle school with great difficulty: he does not like those subjects. On the other hand, at the Academy of Fine Arts, in Via di Ripetta in Roma (1956-1959), he immediately stands out for his talents.

Unfortunately, his problems in relating to the outside world increases as he grows older. When he is questioned or has exams at school, he vomits and despairs. For this reason, he ends up having to repeat the driving test three times.

Suddenly a glass in my hands

The episode I'm about to tell takes place a few years after I made contact with A.A. and with Al-Anon.

I'm at home, sitting in the room where I still usually rest and watch television.

At the time the furniture was different: there were a white sofa and an armchair, which had been torn to pieces by my kittens. From the walls, small meaningless pictures were staring at me. A furnishing that corresponded, rather than to my needs, to certain bourgeois preconceptions of interior decoration.

In the evening, I am often tired. Not so much due to office work as for the sudden commitments that arise from Mario's life necessities.

Sometimes I rush to the clothes shop he is running in Via del Governo Vecchio, *L'Angelo Azzurro*, to open or close it. Sometimes, during the intervals of my work, instead of having lunch, I rush to bring him the house-keys because often he loses them. Sometimes he is sick and calls for me. Sometimes I have go to the pharmacy on his behalf, because he can't go out, it doesn't matter why.

Sometimes he asks to talk to me because he is just desperate. Sometimes Mamma and I have to go up and down with him to the clinic, the hospital. Between him and us runs an invisible but unstoppable carousel.

To all this, from 1976, we add the time spent on our activities with Al-Anon.

Coming back home relaxed me, just as it still does today: I change my dress, I have dinner, I watch a bit of television. Until the day comes when, after having had dinner and while watching TV, I decide that there is nothing wrong with drinking a finger of cognac. I love distilled spirits.

It is a beautiful bottle. A branded cognac, which I had bought, though I don't remember for which Christmas. Importantly, given the context, the contents are still almost *all* there. Anything wrong? Nothing extraordinary.

One evening, about one month later, I am as usual in front of the television, when suddenly I realize that a glass with a finger of cognac is in my hands and that the bottle is no longer full. I look at the bottom of the glass, and I recalled Wendy's words and the testimony heard by her voice the evening of that distant May of 1974: *"One evening, by chance, I took a sip of whiskey. Thus I became an alcoholic: one sip at a time, one evening after another. Without realizing it. Without wanting it."*

I get up from the couch and, without taking my eyes off the glass, I go to the sink and empty it. The bottle, no. I put it back on the shelf. Twenty years later, I shall be surprised to find it still intact. I had simply forgotten it.

Sometimes my thoughts still go to that evening.
The evening when, on my way back from the University, I decided to fetch my Mother from Al-Anon. What would have happened if I hadn't done it? I do not know. None of us knows what's around the corner that hasn't been taken. But I am grateful to Wendy and to my Higher Power, whoever He is, wherever He is, for having been able to hear and fulfill Wendy's witness.

**_Fifties – Leonella translates for the
Metro Golden Mayer_**

Chapter Three

The Cash

Dad is not there. He must work.
Alessandro is not there. I do not know where he is

Alcoholism, a family disease. The role of Al-Anon.

After the first contact with Al-Anon in 1974, I only seriously started to participate in its activities since the start of 1977.

I soon realize that Al-Anon Program is a tool for attaining balance, one that a family member of an alcoholic rarely commands.

To understand what the Program is, you can think of it as a non-psychiatric and non-medical path for finding healing. One in which you learn the truth about the disease of alcoholism. In addition to new relational mechanisms, especially how the alcoholic's relatives introduce their own imbalances into these relationships. And the way in which this disease grows inside and outside the family, leading to other problems.

Through a spiritually and intellectually guided path, one learns to intervene and make improvements to both one's condition and to that of the whole family.

The official websites of Al-Anon thus explains the role of the Association:

'Our meetings are meetings of peers. The members give neither advice nor suggestions; instead, they share their personal situations and reflect on the infinite experiences gathered in books and pamphlets, thus slowly starting their own gradual recovery. Understanding and accepting that compulsive drinking is a disease, makes serenity possible, and improves relationships within and outside the family. Often, by simply stating this, helps the problematic drinker to start, or continue his rescue program'.

To attend a Group, both in A.A. and in Al-Anon, there are no fees. At the end of the meetings, a collection is made to cover the small expenses such as the coffee and biscuits. That are offered to welcome new members and guests, or during breaks. There is no obligation to attend, nor is there an obligation to speak, nor is any specific identifier data requested.

As mentioned, for doctors and other professionals who wish to collaborate or to acquire a different point of view on issues related to alcoholism, Al-Anon periodically organizes *Public Information meetings*. It is not uncommon for such conferences be held in hospitals or in places of worship. Al-Anon, like A.A., guarantees anonymity.

The first battles: there is a 'Program' also for the Al-Anon members. The Group divides into two factions.

In the first period, during which I am still absent, my Mother translates for the Alcoholics, and is not interested in Al-Anon; considering it a useless Association. At which point a key figure in this tale, a wife of a recovered alcoholic[9] emerged: her name was Abi.

Abi is a woman of the people: she communicates mostly through pats on the back, in an environment that is still predominantly uninformed. Thus her unique approach, for good or ill, works. People chat and exchange information about each other's troubles.

Abi has a small and square shape. She has a face marked by the hardness of life and is endowed with strong charisma. Her life must not have been easy.

Within the Group at the time, a story was circulating: her husband had lent money to someone who didn't want to give it back. Whereupon she went personally to recover the credit, knife in hand, and succeeded.

---

[9] As for A.A., much later we shall come to know that in reality there were already other Al-Anon Groups in Northern Italy.

After Wendy's departure, with Abi leading the Group, the meetings are transformed into long informal chats. Fighting to return to meetings with a theme, thus moving from chatter to the planned Program, isn't an easy task.

The cash is to be defended

Before Mom's and I arrived, Abi hadn't had obstacles in administering the Group in her own way. It was she who kept the 'attendance notebook' and, in exclusivity, the notes of money from the collections. Undisturbed, she had always acted as if the management of the funds was a private right of those who came first.

Soon after our arrival, Abi understands that she will be able to stay in place as a secretary and to hold onto the cash, other than by getting rid of persons like my Mother and me. She fears us because we read, we get informed, we know English, and we also translate the Literature that comes from New York-where the World Service Office (WSO) is based.

Reading at the source, the regulation stating how the Groups should be leaded, I realize that there is something wrong in Abi's management. There is no job rotation, indeed there are no assignments; the secretary is also treasurer, who keeps in the utmost secrecy the data of the 'money book'. Which, at the end of any meeting, surprisingly disappears to the bottom of her capable bag to reappear at the next meeting: always and only in her hands.

My attempt to inform the Group that there is a Conference Approved Literature (CAL) turns me *ipso facto,* into an element of rupture. The Group shares into two factions; on the one hand Abi: who considers the Program for the Al-Anon members as ineffectual. On the other side there is me. I fight to affirm the importance of the Program and to give the few Al-Anon who are there, a process of formation. To increase their autonomy, and become aware of how the organization is (and ought to be) managed.

The process is tiring. A fundamental step is taken when Leonella manages to get hold of and translate the *Steps and Traditions for Al-Anon*, which I, in my turn succeed in introducing into the Program, or in the weekly reflections.

Abi hates us more and more.

Your alcoholic is not sober: "Out of Al-Anon!"

Abi has sensed in Leonella and in me, the worst source of danger for her, and wanders like a beast in a cage, looking for a way to eliminate us.

After winning the battle for the affirmation of a Program, one that must be done by the Al-Anon members for themselves, Leonella and I are forced to commit ourselves to a front that will involve us in a highly emotional way, and that will cost us several months worth of effort and personal tension.

Abi subjects us to public ridicule and intends to exempt us from the Al-Anon Service because, she says, *'your alcoholic is not sober.'* We had to fight with our teeth and nails to convince the Group that if an Al-Anon attends and tries to make the Program, he is a full member, beyond the fact that the alcoholic is actually sober or not.

Al-Anon is strictly for the alcoholic's relatives: "Friends cannot enter!"

As we translate and read, we learn new things. For example, even *alcoholics' friends* can be part of the Al-Anon Groups.

Abi, who distrusts and fears anything coming from Leonella and me, is opposing the inclusion of the alcoholics' friends:

"Al-Anon is only for relatives."

Mom and I know we are right, we know that we are working for those who come in search of help. So we do not give up.

Abi did all she could to dissuade us: even suggesting psychological counseling for my "benefit". One day she and her Deputy Secretary plunged without warning into via Lupatelli, where I had moved to organize the second Roman Al-Anon Group *La Magliana*. On that occasion, I could hear a real maternal sermon:
You are still young; why spending your time in via Lupatelli instead of looking for a nice boy?".

The fight, once again, was won when I was able to bring the official Literature on the topic, to the Group, an Italian translation.
The fact that the news of victory in favor of the alcoholic's friends appears in the *A.A. and Al-Anon Bulletin*, which can give an idea of the importance that those events had at the time for everyone. In the Notiziario n.3, May 1980 [see Appendix] we read: '*All the Al-Anon members, relatives or friends of alcoholics, have the same right to attend the Al-Anon Groups. Moreover, if the alcoholic is active or sober, if he attends or does not attend A.A., is not concerning the Al-Anon Group and the Service in the Group.'*

A.A. asks an Al-Anon for help in managing the Secretariat.

It is 1979, when the second Roman group of alcoholics is formed, and Carlo, the National Secretary for A.A., asks me to go to via Lupatelli both to open the second Al-Anon Group, and to help A.A. with Service Secretary.
The reason they asked a *relative*: that is an Al-Anon, to work for Alcoholics Anonymous is that there were very few of us.
I accepted and as a consequence, moved to that location, leaving Abi in Via Napoli, with her personal management.
The struggle to wrest control of the 'cash' from her, will continue from 1977 to 1981. In those five years three Groups are involved: the one in Via Napoli and the two Groups which arose immediately after, namely the Al-Anon Groups Magliana and Gabriele d'Annunzio.

This problem with Abi will find a resolution only after the first Al-Anon National Assembly, held on 18 October 1981. In a definitive, but upsetting way.

Naive attempts.

We always tried to act peacefully, to not risk upsetting the sobriety of Abi's husband with problems that had to remain internal to Al-Anon. In 1979 three Al-Anon Roman Groups decide that, perhaps to convince Abi to change her behavior; it could be a good idea that Magliana and G. d'Annunzio publish their budgets in the 'A.A. and Al-Anon Newsletter'. Needless to say, the example is not followed by Abi's Group in Via Napoli.

Besides, in the *Statute* of the newly constituted association named *Al-Anon* (4 October 1980), we insert the regulation for the life of the Groups: specifying that the Secretary and the Treasurer-to guarantee the Group, the members and the transparency of the administration-have to be two different members. The Al-Anon Group of Via Napoli signs the Statute, but Abi does not modify her 'money-habits'.

"The accounting notebooks have been thrown away"

At Via Napoli, once I left, everything had remained unchanged. Abi, finally at ease, had continued with her usual conduct.

After the chaos of the first Al-Anon National Assembly (18 October 1981-see paragraphs below), which sees Abi loudly appointed as National Secretary, the Al-Anon members of Magliana and d'Annunzio Groups consult each other.

'At least there was one positive result', everyone was thinking, *'Abi, having been appointed National Secretary, finally will have to leave her Secretary post in Via Napoli, and will have to hand over the collection notebooks'*.

But when the Al-Anon members Magliana and D'Annunzio meet those of Via Napoli and ask for the delivery of the accounting booklets that date back to 1976- that is at Wendy's time -Abi candidly informs them that the notebooks have been *thrown away*.

Then an Al-Anon of Via Napoli, who came with Abi at the appointment, pulls out of his wallet two hundred thousand lire (today about one hundred euros) and delivers them without speaking. It was all.

The Via Napoli Group had met regularly three times a week for five years (1976-1981), and the estimates of the collections we processed were quite different.

The notebooks that *had been thrown away* take away forever the answers to our questions.

I must add that most of the members of Via Napoli were respectable people, and if they never opposed Abi's behavior, it was only because of the misinformation or, worse, because of being intimidated.

Someone thinks about funding.

In this period, in Italy, newspapers start writing about regional funds for groups that deal with drug addictions. A serious matter. As neither A.A. nor Al-Anon can, by statute, accept money from anyone for any reason.

Over the years, respect for the Statutes and Literature prevented us from falling into such errors.

At that time, there have been some discussions on this topic.

"In Milano everyone hates you!"

In the years leading up to 1981, Abi and her husband often travel around Italy to bear witness to the Groups being set up. As —I will find out later, on those occasions in speaking about the work that Leonella and I are doing in Roma, she did so critically, if not negatively: looking for allies *against us;* she is the person who tells it to me in a fit of anger.

As already mentioned I had drafted the Statute of Al-Anon, basing it on the official Literature, and the three existing Groups in Rome approve the inclusion in the text, the clause: according to which a Secretary couldn't also be Treasurer.

In September 1980, a month before going to the Notary, to legally constitute the Association, we hold a meeting on these topics in Via del Teatro Valle. It is on this occasion that Abi, with reference to the prohibition of overlapping tasks, attacks me shouting angrily: *"That's why everyone in Milano hates you"*.

I never understood that sentence, and I still don't understand it today. If everyone in Milano was angry with me for 'that sentence included in the Statute', why did none of the Al-Anon who came from Milano to participate in the Al-Anon Constitution the following month (October 1980), never made mention about their concerns or objections?

Leonella and I do not know how far down we are, of having drunk the bitter chalice of Abi's hatred, as she is seeing her eggs broken in the basket.

We had made the suggestion to legally establish Al-Anon from Carlo. As founding members, we simply accept those who are willing to participate. I am given the task of Coordinating Secretary for the simple reason that I am just doing it. Wanting to expand our works to the rest of Italy, we call an Al-Anon from Senigallia, one from Castions di Strada, two from Milano, and we also enjoy the participation of Peter from the United States. Peter is a priest, and is attending the Al-Anon Group of Via Napoli with great interest.

On 4 October 1980, before the Notary Urbano Fascia, the same Notary who had assisted Alcoholic Anonymous, the *Association for Relatives and Friends of Alcoholic Anonymous – Al-Anon,* is established.

The 'A.A. and Al-Anon newsletter' first issue (1980).

The first issue of the monthly *Newsletter A.A. and Al-Anon* is a typewritten sheet.

Carlo and Robertino of A.A., often talked and argued about the need for a news bulletin to link the Groups and keep us up-to-date with each other, but none of us had a clear idea of how to proceed, and perhaps we also feared we did not have sufficient strength to carry the task forward. One evening I take a sheet of paper and type it on both sides. I write *'Notiziario'* on it, and I bring it to Carlo for approval: he is delighted about it. Thus was born the first *A.A. and Al-Anon Newsletter* (see Appendix). One year later, the A.A. and Al-Anon Newsletter would be divided into two separated publications: one for A.A. and one for Al-Anon.   Needless to say: the first issue of the 'Al-Anon News Bulletin'–under Abi's direction- are the famous *'Yellow Sheets'* of 1982, containing only one article by Abi herself (Details of this are given in fifth Chapter).

From March 1980 to the beginning of 1981, before Abi's direction, only twelve editions were worked out jointly by both association and printed. We had dusted off an old mimeograph that forced us to pass the sheets one at a time, and at each exit, we were standing up for several hours. On the other hand the system was absolutely cheap. The text of what we very proudly called *newsletter*, was typed on double rice-sheets. The metal of the typewriter keys broke the first rice sheet, allowing the ink to pass through, and print the characters on the underlying layer. It was an old system that generated a faulty print.

We owe the first dignified and beautiful drawings–yet mortified by the horrible press of the mimeograph-to the collaboration of Umberto First of A.A., a skilled artist (see n.1/1981). We owe him the first serious attempt at designing the cover and the contents. In short: the atmosphere was warming up, and the participation was increasing.

After the first year, the alcoholics are ready to work out their own magazine using their own strengths.

An objection from the General Services.

I would like to take a step back and return for a moment to 1980 to tell an episode that is close to my heart.

In the early months of this year, I decide to write to New York to inform the World Service Office (WSO) of the birth of the second Roman Group, La Magliana; and also to request, on behalf of the Al-Anon Literature Committee, other publications for translation. On that occasion, I proudly inform them of the birth of the *'Monthly Newsletter A.A. and Al-Anon.'*

Before, there had never been direct contact between an Italian Group and the WSO, and I had to write three times before receiving an answer. Finally, when the response arrives, it's a veiled reproach.

The World Service Office responds by saying that *'it would be better if A.A. and Al-Anon had a separate Newsletter.'* They are right. But they cannot imagine how minimal are our forces: in via Lupatelli we are not more than three or four people in all- and how limited is are our economic resources and our experience on the job.

In response, I try to explain the situation, but the bitterness leaks between the lines. As the WSO answers me in a way that takes my breath away. They send me a copy of the latest issue of the American magazine *'Al-Anon Highlights'*. At the center of the front facade is an article dedicated to the work of Al-Anon in Italy and to the work we were doing in via Lupatelli.

It was much more than a prize; it was an example of the correct Al-Anon behavior. The first I received from *overseas*. A way of making decisions that I tried to introduce as a model for my life.

Since then, when someone reacts negatively, I immediately ask myself what wrong I did before, to warrant such a reaction.

The first Al-Anon Literature Committee.

On February 23 1981, Al-Anon formed its own Literature Committee, independent from that of A.A.

Abi is present at the meeting in her capacity of Coordinating Secretary of the National Center, and approves the formation of the Committee. In the 'Yellow Sheets', she will deny this decision, but the documentation proves the contrary. The Committee includes technicians, but also people who do not have specific skills.

Only one year later, we will have a real *technical committee*. The final tasks are the following: Gina of Milano and Maria Grazia translate; Pina of Roma takes care of the shipments together with Enrica, who also keeps the accounts; Leonella translates and coordinates. To me is entrusted the 'last revision.'

At this point in our history, the Pastore Piero Suman (Baptist Evangelical Church located in Via del Teatro Valle 27) granted us the free use of a large empty room, already equipped with shelves, for the storage of our printed Literature. We could not hope for more.

Mario - Via Luigi Lilio.

Our house is big. About 220 square meters. I hear a strange noise in Mario's room. I immediately hurry to see what's going on.

My brother hangs from a rope attached to the ceiling. He is swollen and red, and his legs kick in the void. I scream. My Father rushes to support him by pushing him upwards so that the rope loosens.

The slowness of the reflexes in moments of panic, makes things worse. I only remember that someone (my Mother?), climbing a ladder, cutting the rope. My Father staggers under the sudden weight, but somehow -helped by us- he manages to steady him.

Fortunately, the knot had been badly done, and the only consequence is the headache that broke out for Mario immediately afterward. As usual, we call our faithful doctor and friend Virgilio Pau. He manages to calm Mario's headache with an acupuncture session, which eventually passes with the second session, the day after.

Mario – Traveling to Berlin- August 1963

Chapter Four

Fragments
An offense forever

Dad is not there. He has to work.
Alessandro is not there. I do not know where he is.

Roberto teaches Mario a trick.

In August 1963 one of Mario's friends, who has just taken his driving license and owns a small *Fiat 500*, convinces him to take a trip to Germany. His name is Roberto.

Mario will often recount that his drawings, made on the Ku'damm ground-the most loved avenue in Berlin for gathering artists from all over the world-were the most beautiful ones. And I have no doubt about it. Mario has always been a refined and exasperated aesthete. His friends, mostly belonging to the world of art or antiques, deeply envied him for his artistic qualities. Unfortunately, his few pop-paintings were bought by Roman antique traders for their own homes (Sixties).

Mario realized the portraits of *Theda Bara, Marlene Dietrich* and *Rodolfo Valentino*, all made with sequins, pearls, bracelets and art nouveau belts. Marlene's dress was made entirely with Swarovski degradés crystals. Rodolfo Valentino's dress was made with pieces of small antiques of great value. I still have at home Mario's last work, the *Tarzan*, which remained unfinished.

To stay in Berlin beyond the expected ten days, Roberto devises a brilliant plan: instead of eating they drink. Mario, who had already tried alcohol in Senigallia, shall not stop drinking anymore. Roberto was the older; therefore he was the one who kept the money and was also the only one with the driving-license. Mario, on his return from Berlin, cried and shouted at Roberto for the treatment he had suffered, even though, a posteriori, it is always useless.

September 1963 - Mario while drawing at the Ku'damm in Berlin

Mario and the drugs. The checkered jacket (1958)

Mario and I are sixteen when it turns out he has contracted TB. He has to do a series of treatments for pneumothorax. Mama is desperate: her beloved son, so rich in talent and so young, is haunted by an adverse destiny.

Mario is terrified by the treatment, which at the time was a painful (and impressive) intervention. He cries and despairs. In the end, Mama asks the excellent doctor M. what can be done to calm at least a little of Mario's anguish on the days of the interventions. Doctor M. prescribe a psycho-pharmaceutical. Mario, who is a hypochondriac, since then will never be free from chemical dependence. Several times he told me: *"If I had to fight only alcoholism, I could get out of it. But I can't get rid of chemical drugs."*

In a family like ours – bourgeois and old-fashioned -Mario makes scandal even when he doesn't drink.

One day he goes to the tailor at the end of the street, where Papa has had a gray suit made, and he orders for himself a colorful checkjacket. Dad did not get so angry about the additional cost, as for the colors. A jacket of this kind questioned the life of a good man: a chartered accountant and a serious graduate in Economics and Commerce. He had always dressed in blue and gray, and at most with a slight tone-on-tone pinstripe. On that occassion Mom had to intervene because Dad wanted to beat him.

Shortly after that, he starts going out at night and returning during the early hours. Mamma- who from then on will suffer from insomnia but will never take drugs–always waits for him until he returns home. When back at home, Mario is still in a bad state and very often vomits. Mom assists him until she can put him to bed. Mario's ability to hold up alcohol before staggering is impressive. None of us, however, can understand why he drinks, and none of us think of tying his drinking habit to the word *alcoholism*.

For us, alcoholics are figures from feuilleton, from a popular appendix novel.

My Father thinks only of work and the family. My Mother is a woman who comes from the environment of the Church of the Brothers, fundamentalist and puritan. Alessandro is a university student. I attend an International high school.

We live in a typical environment, if by *typical* we mean people who accept to walk within the social limits of the age; in short, people who *do not disturb*.

Mario, on the other hand, is the absolute *alternative:* and manifests with anger the suffering of his unwanted diversity. Living with him is impossible. When he gets angry, it is better not to be within the reach of dishes. Mario has different habits from or my parents'. Soon, too soon, Dad will adapt to pass him a monthly check, and get him a room outside home, as he insistently asks.

Thus we can find peace at home, but Mario is out of any control. A peace however is shattered by his cries for help, by his terror for the world, by the consequences of the thousand demons that haunt him. Mario is torn by an aesthetic sense that is impossible to satisfy. As well, he is incapable of being the master of himself and his desires.

"You have offended me": Alessandro breaks the family forever (1967)

The relationship between Alessandro and Mario had always been problematic: during our childhood- according to what I remember- they envied each other's qualities. Often they came to blows.

Towards our twelve-thirteen years, Mario and Alessandro begin to go out together: *"Mamma, we go for a walk in Viale Parioli."* After no more than half an hour, usually, the phone is ringing. It is Mario who, crying, asks Mamma for help because Alessandro is mistreating him. At that point, Mamma used to send me to see what was happening, and what was happening was all and nothing. Mario is crying. I console him, then we go back home together.

Alessandro, as always, disappears.

Noting that after his trip to Germany, his younger brother can no longer stop drinking, Alessandro begins to feel guilty for his inability to help him. According to my interpretation, only feelings of guilt can explain the behavior that, ten years later, Alessandro will have towards Mario. Here is what happened and how.

We live in Eur, a neighborhood ten kilometers from Rome. One evening Alessandro decides to offer the ticket for the *Teatro dei Servi,* to Mario. It doesn't seem real at home. Can it be that they have finally started to get along? The brothers dress up and leave. They take the car of Alessandro, and from the Eur, they move to the center of Roma.

Everything is good. They enter the theater. Still okay. The show begins and shortly after, the real drama also begins. According to Mario, the show is too stupid; he gets up and leaves. Alexander, the following morning, proclaims: *"It's either me or Mario."*

He had felt offended because of the conduct of his younger brother, who had left the show 'he had been paying for'.

It sounds silly, absurdly trivial overall because Alessandro is not an alcoholic: yet he broke the family He broke it, starting with that evening. No mercy for anyone. No mercy forever.

Mario and I, between the twenty-fifth and thirty-fourth years of our lives, did not notice it much, because Alessandro spent most of that period traveling abroad. But when he returns to Italy in 1976, the reality of that decision on that fateful day (at the drama), falls upon us, and for the sixteen long years that was to follow[10].

In those sixteen years, there shall not be, for Mario and for me, either a Christmas, a New Year or a birthday party or any other family celebration. Alessandro used to go home triumphantly, followed by his wife and the little children. I, on the other hand, left home and went to see my twin brother with a small pan wrapped in a cloth, so as not to disperse the heat. We spent our time together, but never

---

[10] Till Mario's death in 1992, November 29

were really happy. In this way, he and I celebrated Christmas and the New Year. Even Sundays, and of course, birthdays. He and I. Alone. Without family, for sixteen long years.

Only when Alessandro, for divine reasons, wasn't able to come, the home's doors were reopened to Mario.

For this behavior, I scolded my Father for a long time. Dad usually stammered something about his grandchildren, and the talk ended there.

Mario suffered so much for this too. He never knew his brother's children.

In my opinion, as already mentioned, Alessandro broke his relationship with Mario, probably to remove the feelings of guilt which affected him after the infamous trip to Berlin. In his mind–I believe–he had failed to give his younger brother the valid support to overcome his alcoholism.

He took the short and wrong path: removing from his life the object of his imaginary faults, as most people often do.

Perhaps he was unaware that what we bury in the unconscious, remains a living matter. An ember that whilst forgotten in the depths of our being, can slowly burn everything. The break of Alessandro with his younger brother, in my opinion, was reinforced by the trauma that he suffered as a child, at the sight of the screaming bundles that *had taken away his mother's love.*

I know that Alessandro, between his thirty and thirty-fifth years, while abroad, tried to talk to a psychological counselor because of these experiences, as one of my family members told me at the time.

In interpersonal relationships, according to my understanding, I do not believe there are faults, but rather *concurrent causes*, and only by clearing these causes, shall will be able to forgive ourselves as well as others, as a way of repairing our emotional and relational pains.

If Alessandro had understood these things, instead of forever breaking by the family denying his support to everyone, maybe things would have gone differently.

Alessandro will also tear me from his heart: the other screaming bundle, but these are different stories and have nothing to do with alcohol, or maybe they do.

The iguana

Among so many imbalances and pains, Mario always kept another incredible gift: he knew how to arouse laughter. His sense of humor and irony was incredibly acute. Mixed with his perception of people's shortcomings. He had the ability to make anyone laugh in an irrepressible way. His imitations, whether the victim was himself, a passerby or a friend, were hilarious. His friends, as long as he had any, sought him out also for this, because he was a fun person, and even for this reason they envied him.

Mara, one of the very first A.A. of Via Napoli, still laughing told me when she and Robertino of Via Napoli went to see Mario to make the *Twelfth Step*[11]. Mario kindly invited them to sit down and then calmly, pulled out a little tray full of 'grass', asking them for a favor. Naturally, they did not accept, but Mario, making the situation paradoxical, succeeded in making them laugh so much that they still remember it.

I also remember the hilarity he aroused when explaining the dialogue between him and a poor policeman. The officer wanted to fine Mario because, at Villa Borghese, he was roaming with an iguana, with a collar made of diamonds, and a gold chain: all of which were obviously fake.
Crazy? Maybe. Or maybe he was just desperate for the limelight.

---

[11] A.A. 12th Step: *Having had a spiritual awakening as the result of these steps, we tried to carry this message to alcoholics, and to practice these principles in all our affairs.*

Mario had an incredible bearing on the environment. Even though he was only a meter and seventy-two tall, whatever he wore, it always seemed very stylish.

One day, in via Frattina, two ladies approached him to ask if he was a Belgian prince. He was wearing only a linen shirt, a pair of trousers and an old leather bag thrown over his shoulders.

Beautiful scarves.

It is springtime. Mario lives in via dei Banchi Nuovi, and I go to see him. He's knitting. Someone may think: *"Well he must be gay."*

Well, if he is a gay or not, isn't important here. Mario, when weaving the threads of wool, *was also painting*. I've never seen such beautiful poly-chromes. I still have photos of these works somewhere. Mario is probably the only artist I know, who can create something beautiful by using woolen threads. Since this artistic medium is very demanding.

He was knitting, and he was sad, sad and sad:
"If at least I could sell a scarf!"
It tormented him, the fact of not being able to get a job, to earn money, and becoming financially independent of the family.

Suddenly I grab a scarf: *"Now I'll try myself. You'll see that I can!"* I was determined. At the time, there was the practice of leaving small things to the shopkeepers in return for a deposit. They only paid, if the items got sold.

I go through all of via dei Banchi. *'No'* from the first store, *no* from the second, *no* from the third. *No, no, no.* In the end, I enter a little shop that seems really suitable: *"Excuse me, I thought maybe you could keep this scarf... only in storage... I don't want anything... Okay, I'll tell you: it's for a person who is not well. I would just go home and tell him that someone took this scarf in storage. Please!"*

The guy looks at me without expression all the time. He shakes his head and keep silence. In the end, I have to leave. As I walk back, my brother's despair becomes mine. They were beautiful scarves, so it became a day devoid of hope and joy. For my brother it would have been enough to know that one of his scarves had been put on display. Not even sold: just showcased.

That evening I had to pay a thousand years of pain. I had to go up, knock, enter, and tell him that there was no shop-window for his scarves. Mario looked at me. He told nothing. He just looked at me. I still remember his glance.

Indeed, that shopkeeper had no idea the goodness he could have done by taking at least one of those beautiful scarves, even without paying it and just throwing it somewhere.

He certainly didn't imagine the pain he was giving me, if not to my brother. For forty years later, it would still be alive in my heart.

They were beautiful scarves. I had asked the shopkeeper to take only one of them, without paying.

Mario looked at me. He said nothing. He just looked at me. I still remember his glance.

Mario faces the world of entertainment.

Mario had had several opportunities to enter the world of art and theater. Which he squandered by presenting himself under intoxication.

I remember when I went to see the drama 'In Morte di un Papa' staged by Fiorenzo Fiorentini. On that occasion, he had to take care of the scenes and costumes. When the lights were switched off, and the red curtain opened, a whisper of wonder rose from the stalls: Mario had managed to create a magnificent silver scene. The article of December 16, 1972, of the *Avanti*, which I still retain, hadn't been kind with the actors, but thus concluded *'The costumes, very varied and rich in fanciful nuances, are by Mario d'Alatri.'*

Mario was radiant: critics rarely notice the costume designer or the set designer, and he felt as if he was entered into *the bunch of the elected.* When Fiorentini contacted him again, he presented himself after having too many drinks.

In 1973, the year of the meeting with Alcoholics Anonymous, he was working as a costume designer for Vitaliano Brancati in 'La Governante'. Later he was 'assistant production designer' of Umberto Bertacca in 'the Coriolano' and assistant-set-designer in the very famous 'Orlando Furioso' directed by Luca Ronconi.

But at work, in order to summon the courage to face people and take responsibility, he had to drink.

Until one day no one called him anymore.

Disturbing episodes in Perugia.

Mario seemed to be haunted by a demon who envied his talents.

My Mother and I always suffered because Mario was the victim of many unfortunate experiences.

Like a typical episode, I'm going to speak about the one that happened in Perugia.

After the death of Pietro and Elisa, I had managed to convince him- with difficulty-to come with me to visit the newly established A.A. Group in Perugia. Ada and Lino, Al-Anon and A.A., had warmly invited him. In those days Mario was again trying to detox, and was absolutely sober.

The train journey is short and peaceful. Then something happens that I still can't make sense of. As we get off the train, we bump into a little man with a railway-man's uniform. I don't remember why we talked, but he immediately invites us to enter an Office in front of the platform. As soon as we enter, he offers a drink to Mario. Not to me; *only* to him. Mario said *'no, thanks!'* But the railwayman insists. At that point the scene become grotesque: Mario starts to run around the table which is the only piece of furniture in the room, while the man chases him. I am paralyzed.

As God wills it, we both run away from that room. Unfortunately, the problems are not over.

On foot, we walk towards the center of the city, and in the central square we are frozen by another dramatic scene. One of the hotels had caught fire, and one person is hanging outside a window on the fourth- floor. We run away from there.

The hospitality of Lino and Ada is affectionate but Mario,of course, didn't want to return to Perugia any more.

Chapter Five

From the first publications to the Yellow Sheets

Dad isn't there. He has to work.
Alessandro is not there. I do not know where he is.

Leonella - First Al-Anon pamphlets: A.A. lends us the money.
First Al-Anon book: a Typography helps us.

In March 1980, with the money lent by A.A., the first five Al-Anon pamphlets are printed in a very economical way:
'The story of Luisa', 'To the parents of an alcoholic', 'A guide for the alcoholic family', 'Do you love an alcoholic' and 'Liberation from despair'.
To save money, I get the price-list written by hand, by an alcoholic who has excellent handwriting; then we distribute via photocopy.
In the meantime I read the A.A. Service Manual[12] - which is still not translated. Here I understand that to save money, the Association must become the publisher of its own Literature.
In March 1981, we officially give life to the Al-Anon Literature Committee, and we decide to publish our first book: 'The Dilemma of the Alcoholic Marriage'.
To orientate me and to be more certain of what I would have to do, I make an appointment with the Publishing House of the 'Great Book' of A.A. Thus, I realize that was right in thinking that printing a book through a publishing house would be far too costly for us. With the risk of becoming heavily indebted.

---

[12] The Service Manual contains the instructions of the WSO, for the creation in one's own country; of a *communication network* between Groups, called *structure*. At the head of which is there is an Assembly, in which all the Groups are represented.

So I go directly to various printers, which fortunately are numerous in my neighborhood. I take the original American book with me, to make sure that they can accurately reproduce the same typographic appearance. I get estimates from three or four typographers and then gather the Literature Committee.

We choose our printer on a price basis, and our choice of printer will prove to be correct, because the printer will become a sympathizer of Al-Anon; and will go onto help us in many ways. The Typographer gives us the price for 2000 copies, but we only print a thousand books, under the agreement that if we can order another thousand within a short period, the price will remain the one first agreed. If instead, we do not succeed, nothing will be due.

Immediately we ask the Groups to book copies, so to make a commitment with the Printer. The Groups responded with enthusiasm and with sufficient orders.

The Typography was indeed giving us credit but, in any case, we needed an advance of 500,000 lire (today 250 euro).

The newly established National Center has no cash at all. So I tried to ask for a loan from the Al-Anon Group of Via Napoli, but the answer is negative.

At last a member of Al-Anon pays the advance for the Typography, renouncing the opportunity to go to Zurich; where he had decided to take part in an Al-Anon Conference which also had to be attended by Lois. For which an expenditure of 500,000 lire was planned.

The sacrifice made by that Al-Anon member, allows us to print our first book despite all sorts of doubts and fears, but also with so much enthusiasm and satisfaction.

At the time, I had no experience in printing, so I feared that something could go wrong. It is therefore with great concern that I give, as a sample, a copy of the American edition to our Typographer to print our first book.

I like the cover very much, and I am afraid they aren't able to reproduce it 'identically', with the same colors. I tell the printer that before printing, I want to see the proof. That night I do not close my eyes: 'how can they reproduce the same red? And if the green changes? Because if one of the two is different, maybe it punches with the other one'.

The next morning, at eight, I am already at the Printer. Thanks to God, the colors are exactly the same. It was such a happy day that I still remember it with great pleasure.

The first book of Al-Anon, 'The Dilemma of the Alcoholic Marriage', sees the light on July 1981. And after the first book, we reprinted the pamphlets, identical to the original American version. The time for photocopying was over.

Extras in the Assembly

While Mom goes on with the problems of translating and printing, I am committed to creating the Structure in Italy. I could not possibly imagine a cataclysm awaits the first Al-Anon National Assembly, scheduled for October 18, 1981.

After reading the A.A. Service Manual, Leonella had asked the WSO for the 'Al-Anon Service Manual', which gave us a reasonably accurate idea of how a national structure has to be organized.

Although we haven't had the time to translate it, we include in the agenda of the Assembly, the vote for the approval of the essential elements of the network through which to connect. Familiarly known as the *structure*.

The *A.A. and Al-Anon Monthly Newsletter* reports the agenda scheduled for our first Assembly:

Agenda for the First National Assembly
(extract)

• Financial Situation: Report of the National Center and Report of the Al-Anon National Committee for Literature...
• Election of the National Secretary, the Treasurer and the Board of Directors...
• Appointment of Regional Representatives...

In my capacity as Secretary-founder (see Appendix-By-laws' extract) with the help of the Al-Anon Group La Magliana, I had summoned all the Al-Anon Groups at the time, according to the communications received, the number was about a dozen.

Thanks to the reading of the Manual, sent to us by New York, the base of the Al-Anon structure is ready and, in this first Assembly, we have planned to appoint a Representative for each Region (or area) and the first voted-National Secretary.

As things go, it seems that something upsetting and inexplicable *had* to happen. In the room of via Lupatelli 62, where people are already sitting, some women enter screaming and protesting that they represent Al-Anon Groups of which, until that moment, no one has ever heard about.

Extras? I do not know. For none of us ever saw them again. In short: the Assembly was sunk among screams and cries launched by those secretaries. Shocked by that violent assault, and not prepared to face such an incident, I leave the Assembly together with some of the other Al-Anon.

The screaming women, as soon as we left the room, loudly voted for Abi as National Secretary for the following year, shortly after, the Assembly was over.

As a result of this incident, we could not relate to anyone on the year of work, nor could we proceed to vote for the *regional representatives:* the foundation upon which we had to build the *structure*.

On the same evening of October 18, Abi asked me for approximate deliveries. I understood what I could give her was not of great interest to her, and my presence was no longer needed.

But what was the trigger for those events? I can only hypothesize.

My determination to introduce the Program, to include the Steps and Traditions for Al-Anon, to allow friends of alcoholics to join the Groups, to allow the Al-Anon members to serve, even if the alcoholic was not sober, on top of that, *my battle for the transparent administration of funds*, were strongly opposed by Abi.

Precisely at that time, the Lazio-Region was starting to allocate money for 'organized structures', which had to allocate that money to bring help to people with addictions. Leonella and I, needless to say, were amongst those who were in defense of the Al-Anon principles, and had sided against this approach.

Not even a month after that cataclysm, Abi, pushed by Leonella, is forced to gather the National Council and to give the approval, that was denied during the Assembly: the *structure* is voted and approved, and the Council agrees to appoint the Group Representatives and District Representatives.

The Council agrees, but the record was thrown at the bottom of a drawer and the structure, once again, remained only on paper.

Abi defended her ground like a predator.

Between struggles, reconsideration, meetings and discussions, the structure was to be launched only on October 1986 by the Al-Anon National Center in Milano.

The chaos of the first Assembly (18 October 1981) caused a delay of over five years in the construction of the 'Al-Anon structure' nationwide in Italy.

A phone call: "Leonella, keep quiet. Now there is money for everyone".

A few days after the Assembly, Abi calls Mamma and, literally tells her: *"Leonella, keep quiet. Now there is money for everyone!"*

Abi has realized that she has been wrong twice. The first time in evaluating the money in storage; the second one in evaluating Leonella, although she knows her very well.

The Al-Anon structure -for its support- is expected to receive money from the Groups (a percentage of their cash surplus); but the mechanism hasn't yet been improved. For the simple reason that no money could be requested before the first Assembly[13].

Conclusion: there is no money in the coffers of the Center.

Second gigantic mistake: Leonella is the last person in the world to whom Abi could give such a speech, and even today it surprises me.

On that occasion, I realize that Abi maybe charismatic, maybe even smart, but certainly not farsighted.

Mom doesn't answer Abi. She just hangs the phone.

After discovering that the National Center is without a penny, Abi is now turning to the Literature Committee's cash; the plan is to merge the Literature Committee's money with that of the National Center.

It would have been an inadmissible administrative error, because the revenues of a specific administrative sector must balance its debts. And, if the balance is positive, the surplus has to finance the new prints. In any case, mixing two administrations can only lead to administrative chaos.

The newly elected National Center led by Abi, burdens the Committee with useless paper work for most of the following year, whose real purpose was to aid the unification of the Literature administration into the National Center. Leonella, aware of the administrative damage that would result, always opposes. For those who undertake to take on debts to manage a production, must be able to manage the inputs to repay those debts.

In that first year, another dramatic episode takes place, confirming that only the realization of the *structure* could have saved Al-Anon from a big confusion.

---

[13] In fact, to activate the *mechanism* we were waiting for the first Assembly of October 18, 1981, which was to be wrecked by of the intervention of the unknowns.

An alcoholic points the gun at Leonella: "I kill you!"

Determined to realize the structure as suggested by the WSO, despite the opposition of Abi, during that first year of *Abi's reign;* Leonella convenes an *open meeting* on the topic of 'structure', of both A.A. and Al-Anon Roman Groups. She believes that the presence of the Alcoholics can be helpful, given they have already built their structure and therefore they can give us helpful input.

There was a remarkable participatory response. The hall of the Church that welcomes people, is packed.

The presentation of the meeting takes place orderly, till my mother takes up the microphone and starts speaking.

Suddenly her voice is buried by someone shouting at her from the bottom of the room.

An alcoholic stands up and whilst aiming a revolver to her, shouts *'I kill you!'*.

It is a new setup by Abi. The man is Vauro, her alcoholic husband. She thought of *throwing* him at Leonella to scare her, and -who knows- maybe getting rid of her. In fact Abi is frightened by the *structure,* because she understands that she cannot carry on as usual under it.

Panic breaks out in the room. Vauro's friends throw themselves at him, to prevent him from doing something irreversible and stupid.

Luckily there were no consequences, and Leonella continues to work to spread the culture of the *Al-Anon structure* in Italy, as suggested by the WSO. Together with her, are her great allies Marisa of Dolo and Gina of Milano.

Mom, myself and others had always been worrying about the *sobriety* of Abi's husband. So working to avoid clashes would have been necessary. We feared the internal fights of Al-Anon could in some way affect his sobriety. On the other hand Abi, on that occasion, to achieve her goals, had jeopardized the sobriety of Vauro, pushing him to take a revolver in his hands.

For Mom and me however, the problems are not yet over.

Waiting for us there are still the *Yellow Sheets* and the *Meeting of Padova;* and Abi wants to burn us alive, and throws her tongues of fire farther and more menacingly.

'The Yellow Sheets' (June 1982)' - Leonella and Laura are dangerous subjects for Al-Anon. They also inform New York about it.

After the appointment of the first Literature Committee[14] and after the 1981 Assembly, Abi suggests to Leonella during a phone conversation, to recompose the Literature Committee with members who have the qualifications to fully collaborate. She first resigns of her own will.

From the facts that follow, it is easy to understand that Abi resignation from the Literature Committee is only because she cannot afford sink a Committee in which she herself is a part of.

On January 1982, following Abi's suggestions, Leonella recomposes the Literature Committee and informs Abi that everything had been performed as she had requested: at last all those who are taking part on the Committee have specific tasks. Privileged assignments are now over. The translations are done well, and are made at a rapid pace. The *Al-Anon culture* spreads far and wide in our small world.

In 1982 the National Center, notwithstanding the protests of Abi, appoints Leonella as a Delegate to the World Service Conference in New York. The meeting will gather two delegates from each country, from many parts of the world.

Abi is furious, and not only because of the nomination of Leonella, but that she can no longer get the money of Via Napoli, and the National Center is as broke as its Groups; indeed, it has zero income and zero growth. The maneuver to unify the Literature Committee's and the National Center accounts by Abi having failed, Leonella is increasingly appreciated for her efforts.

---

[14] February 1981

Abi has no peace until she produces another *brilliant* idea. And so the *Yellow Sheets* come to life.

Laura has just passed the responsibility of the old '*A.A. and Al-Anon Newsletter*' to an alcoholic for A.A. and to an A.A.'s relative for Al-Anon.
But when the new *Alcoholics Anonymous Bulletin* comes out, inside there is a *Supplement* containing news from the Al-Anon world. The Supplement is named '*Here Al-Anon*'.

Those sheets, which bear the signature of Abi as National Secretary, and will become infamously known as '*The Yellow Sheets*': being printed on yellow paper, they are entirely and exclusively dedicated to Laura and Leonella.

Here is a list of its affirmations:
[Laura and Leonella have no official duties inside Al-Anon; they act like crazy splinters without any endorsement; they are harmful to Al-Anon; they have taken and are taking independent initiatives apart from the central management. Laura had the crazy idea of promoting contacts between the Al-Anon Lazio Groups, which led to the Al-Anon Lazio Intergroup. And, last but not least, no one has ever appointed Leonella as a Delegate to New York (we have seen in the previous paragraphs that Abi had instead voted in favor of Leonella)].

Finally, Abi writes that Laura and Leonella must get out of Al-Anon. To make the situation even more serious was that the Sheets, as a Supplement of the 'A.A. Newsletter', was sent not only to all the Al-Anon Groups, but also to all the A.A. Groups! A few alcoholics with whom Leonella and I had a strong friendship with, were deeply disturbed.
The resentment and anger caused by Abi for the events described up to now had erupted, infecting everything and everyone like a poison. Abi understood-as noted-that with the structure, the spreading of the Steps, Traditions and Service Concepts and with the increas-

ing number of the Groups, Al-Anon was going beyond her organizational capacity to control. My Mother and I, as a defence and as a proof that all the initiatives we had taken, were complying with the guidelines suggested by Al-Anon in the world, immediately translate an extract from the 'Al-Anon Service Manual'. However, as sociology teaches us, it is no coincidence that stigmatization dies hard.

The Yellow Sheets: the answers were never published

The Yellow Sheets were the only occasion in which Abi took care of applying the 'Al-Anon WSO' translating the text in English
In the answer sent back to her on 10 November 1982, by the diplomatic and untiring Mary Ann K. we read among other things: *... it is sad that you could not resolve your differences of opinion without bringing this to the attention of the Groups. This type of conflict could deeply affect a structure - in its bud ... Leonella has submitted a proposal for structure for Al-Anon in Italy* [note: the 'structure' sunk on 18 November 1981]... *on the opinion of the International Coordination Committee, it is a good plan to follow...'*

The Committee for Literature, on 30 July 1982, officially replied to them.
Moreover two Counselors (Maria Grazia and Elsa) responded personally, and finally my Mother and I also answered separately. *These answers were never disclosed; neither was the response sent by the WSO to Abi revealed [see Appendix].*

The correspondence between Leonella and New York is censored. The WSO is spiritually dangerous.

Whilst this was taking place, once appointed as National Secretary, Abi again imposes herself on the communications between Leonella and New York.

On 16 May 1982, in the letter addressed by Leonella to Mary Ann K., we read:

[...] *The 'A.A. Office' in via Lupatelli puts aside the letters for us coming from the 'Al-Anon WSO', and then gives them to Abi who wants to read them before allowing us to get hold of them [...] The consequence is that I'm receiving your letters late months. Moreover, if you include forms or other sheets, perhaps because she [Abi] does not know English, I rarely receive them* [Leonella explains she has received only two communications from New York in six months. Then she continues talking about the 'structure']. *Now, in Italy, we have about 45 Groups, and they are certainly enough to give life to a 'structure' [...] I send you under a separate cover, an extract from the 'Handbook of Guidelines' that Laura has translated*[15]*, to send it to all our Groups. The National Council chaired by Abi, has however decided that it is 'not yet time' to share all this information with the Groups [...]'*

But Leonella is far from surrendering, and continues: *'[...] so the Literature Committee, not being able to put the Handbook on the list of publications of the National Center, has decided to put it on the list of the publications of the Al-Anon Lazio Intergroup. This way, at least in Lazio District, it shall spread'.*

In trying to defend her untenable position, Abi resorts to measures, which amounts to spiritual terror. A group chaired by her, regarding the Manual and Structure, writes and publishes the following:

'The structure, as suggested by the World Service Office of New York, is a spiritual danger for our Association.'

The Padova Meeting (September 1982): Abi insists on throwing Leonella out of Al-Anon.

[Abi uses the Meeting in Padova to attack Leonella again. The Meeting, without any warning, and at the last moment, is declared to be

---

[15] It was my only translation. I worked in the Literature Committee almost always as a proofreader and text reviser.

an *Extraordinary National Assembly*, to discuss two unanticipated topics: the Al-Anon structure and Leonella's behavior. As Leonella writes about it:

'*The atmosphere, prepared by the Yellow Sheets, was overheated. I understood that they wanted to oust me, and I was worried because we had not yet been able to communicate to anyone all that we had elaborated and learned about 'structures', and how important they were. So in a rush I wrote the 'Proposal for an Al-Anon structure in Italy'. Late into the night an alcoholic named Anna helped me by dictating the notes I typed, and also helped me in remembering the main points.*

I thought that if the Meeting in Padova had to be our[16] last chance to get our voices heard; at least the outline of the structure would be spread. Some people from the National Center did everything they could to stop me from distributing that note; and in order to do it, I had to impose myself with all my energy...'

Indeed, those internal conflicts, as well as the previous ones- whose reading, we hope, finally makes the events clear - influenced the misunderstandings between Milano and Roma.

But not even through the Padova-Meeting, was Abi able to sink the proposals, on how to set up the structure of Al-Anon in Italy.

Mario - Via dell'Agnello

The worst suicide attempted by Mario is the one which follows the meeting with a psychologist. We were the ones who convinced him to meet that particular doctor.

At the time Mario was living in Via dell'Agnello.
He went to the appointment but left the session half-way through. Later on, my brother told us the doctor was a feeble and simple man,

---

[16] When Leonella says 'ours', she refers to the Al-Anon members who fought with her in favor of spreading the official Literature, and therefore also of the realization of the Structure.

and when he had analyzed him, he learnt that he was a man with a certain complex. Mario never revealed all the events of that session; but at a certain point during the session, and with no prior cause, the psychologist had thrown him out of the door.

The requests for more details remained unanswered.
What I do know is that the day after Mario called home saying he was sick. I was at work in the Bank, and my mother at that time didn't want to call me
Mom, entering his home, found blood splashed up to the ceiling. Mario had tried again to kill himself. This time he had cut an artery.
After that, we stopped proposing him to go to such sessions.

Chapter Six

Fragments
Ernesto meets Al-Anon

Dad is there, and it's important.

Rene' meets Al-Anon.

Rene', as my Mother always was calling Dad, sounds like a snobbish Gallicism. Instead, it was only the abbreviation of my Dad's name, in a specific Italian dialect (Ernesto – *Rene*sto).

But let's go back to our story.
Rene' is about ten years old, and his classmates call for him from the street: *"Rene', come down!"*
But Rene' always answers *"No. I cannot. I have to study"*.
When Rene' comes home from school, grandmother Anna, his mother; uses to take off his hob-nailed shoes. As once upon a time, needy people were doing: shoes have to last for years. They have to be worn only to school.

Grandfather Domenico, the husband of grandmother Anna, was a skilled shoemaker. Many years before he had left for America, looking for a job to feed his wife and their three children. Domenico sent money when he could, until one day he did not post anything anymore.
Repeatedly invited by her husband to face the sea-crossing with their children, to unite the family across the Atlantic. However grandma Anna always refused to do so because, not being able to swim: she was terrified of crossing the sea.

She did prefer to deal with her uncertain fate as a wardrobe mistress at the home of certain noble people; as she boasted, in trying to defend her social status - rather than getting on a ship.

Dad had a sister and a brother: Nennè and Giulio.
Nennè married a young and friendly clerk, employed in a cloth shop in via Frattina, and she was happy about the decision. Uncle Giulio, as soon as he could, took the driving license and became a truck driver. But my father, endowed with a strong will and being brilliant, was industrious in various jobs and was able to pay for his own education in accountancy. At a times when accountancy was viewed as a highly formative subject. After the diploma, he succeeded in getting hired by a large company and was able to finance his university education.

"I used to work all day," Papà said several times: *"and in the evening, not to fall asleep, I would study standing next to the bed, so when I fell asleep, I fell onto the bed."* In the last two years of University, he was also a lieutenant in the Army.

Dad graduated without delay with full marks.
He will live his youth under the shadow of the myth of the 'strong man': a social representation of his time. Which was a possible by-product of Mussolini's leadership. Then during the war, he got married, had children, and devoted himself to his family.

If you now feel as if you wanted to throw the first stone at this man because he could not accept a son with overly sensitive traits: a son who used to wear eccentric clothes instead of playing football, a son who was wearing bright colored jackets instead of gray ones? Alright, then, you are free to throw that stone. But I shan't.

Having been involved in the slow unfolding of these events, in the course of my family's life, I'll rather speak about 'concomitant causes': not of 'guilt'. Dad and Mario were both unlucky in equal and opposite ways. So the day when Mamma was able to bring Papa to an Al-Anon meeting in Via del Teatro Valle, it came as a blessing.

When that small number of people representing the Group succeeded in making him understand that a gay person is someone who has an additional hurdle to face in life, to those which are faced by others. They succeeded in making him understand that he had not generated a monster, but a person who has a disease called *alcoholism.* I saw tears running down my father's face.

His relationship with Mario changed. But it was too late to really help my twin brother. However, that time Dad was present. And it was important.

Chapter Seven

From New York to Milano

Dad isn't there. He has to work.
Alessandro is not there. I do not know where he is.

Leonella -The New York meeting is moving. They hand me the copyright for the book: 'A day at a time in Al-Anon' (20/23 September 1982).

We are at the end of 1982 and 'One day at a time' (ODAT), translated by Gina of Milano, after an accurate revision, is ready for printing. However, we are missing both the copyright from New York and the money for the printing.

Thus we resort to the ploy already used for the previous book (see Chapter 5 - 'Leonella': the first publications). We write to the Groups asking them to book the copies of ODAT, they are willing to buy. We inform them that, if we can reach a certain number of orders, the Printer-conquered by our enthusiasm and trusting in our editorial skills and our precision in payments-will give us the credit for the printing of the first two thousand books. Then, once the first money arrives, another thousand will be printed at the same cost. In short, we put in place the same procedure already used for 'The Dilemma of the Alcoholic Marriage.'

We are close to the New York meeting and I am confident that once there, by carefully engaging the relevant parties, I will be able to speed up the procedure to get the permission to print.

While I'm preparing for my first overseas travel, without calling the Board meeting and without explanations, two members of the National Center decide to replace me and to send as Delegate to New York a newcomer: who does not know English and, being new, does not even know anything about our Literature[17]. After a new set of bitterly fought conflicts, I am confirmed as a Delegate, and in September I leave for New York with Patricia.

Indeed, the WSO in New York hadn't accepted the change, this late in the assignment and outside the envisaged channels.

The Meeting with the representatives of the WSO -which in the meantime had followed our ups and downs, through the contacts with the Literature Committee- is thrilling.

They were waiting for me, to deliver in person, the copyright for ODAT. The enthusiasm and surprise are such, that from New York, I immediately call Roma to inform the Printer that he can start printing. In New York, we will leave each other with a warm 'goodbye', given that the Heads of the Conference, are in charge for two years and, as a Delegate, I too had to be in charge for two years.

Leonella-The National Center is transferred to Milano: "Finally a hope" (October 1982).

Shortly afterward, with the 1982 elections, the newly elected Coordinating Secretary was Vincenza of Milano, and we heard they wanted to move the headquarters to Milano. I was relieved. We would finally understand each other.

In particular, I felt the responsibility for the storage of books and pamphlets, and I would have had other people to ask for advice. I realized that one risk was to print too many copies of a booklet or a book, and then to not succeed in selling them.

I was really confident that someone in Milano could have helped us in dealing with this financial problem. 'And then-I thought- they

---

[17] With moderate tones, Leonella refers to Abi's attempt to appoint an alternate delegate instead of her for New York. On that occasion, meeting and voting were not valid, as none of the Councilors was summoned by Abi but one. The WSO, for its part pointed out the failure in complying with the required procedures and times. Abi, eventually disavowed her vote in favor of the appointment of Leonella (March 24, 1982, see Appendix).

are more numerous than us, and it will be easier to find someone who can help us with the planning of the Literature production.'

I had already planned to involve the future District Representatives in the decisions to be made and, after the experiences I had during the period with Abi, I was looking forward to talking about the problems of the Literature with other Al-Anon friends.

After reading the first beautiful letter sent by Vincenza to the Groups, I breathed a sigh of relief. "Now–I told myself and to my friends–the problems are over[18]."

Leonella - Milano, Assembly 10/12 December 1982: "They forbid me from reporting on the New York meeting. I am informed that my assignments are going to finish."

On 10 December 1982, I went to Milano to attend the first annual Al-Anon Assembly led by Vincenza.

I was full of enthusiasm. Naturally, I had prepared a report on the meeting of the General World Service, held in New York three months before (20/23 September 1982).

Then something totally unexpected happens again: nobody asks me to report to the Assembly about the world meeting in New York. I am made to understand that, soon, my role as Literature Coordinator will end; and that as a Delegate, my two-year mandate is to be suspended. It is true that they asked me the Written Report on the New York Meeting and I immediately delivered it. But it is also true that 'it was never released'.

Since the main point of those who wanted to dismantle the Literature Committee and transfer it to Milano, was that a coordinator, after two years, must leave and cannot be reelected, we are dismayed to write to New York and explain the situation.

---

[18] On January 9, 1983, Leonella writes to Vincenza a letter that reflects her dedication, her hopes and her love for Al-Anon. She puts at her disposal all the information that is in her possession, and the help she can give. But once again, something very different happened from what was hoped for (Appendix- Correspondence).

From New York they reply with messages addressed to both Roma and Milano, explaining that the Coordinators lasted, as a rule, for 'three years', and when a Coordinator has a task that is technical in nature, and if things go well, it is good if he or she stays longer.

They explained that they too, had renewed some assignments for several years, for a number of people.
The suggestions, coming from New York were not taken into consideration.
As a last chance, I asked to be heard by the National Center of Milano: insisting that they cannot make such a gesture as to literally 'raze to the ground', the former Literature Committee, without giving explanations for their actions. The National Center promptly grants me a hearing.

Leonella[19] - The meeting with the Arbiters turns into a monologue: no explanations; no answers (January 1983).

In January 1983, I went to Milano accompanied by Maria Grazia. At the meeting we found a Committee of seven or eight people waiting for us. At the start of the meeting, everyone had a negative attitude towards me, but no one explained why.
When I started talking, little by little, I could sense their growing attention and consent. It was as if my listeners were hearing for the first time the story of the Literature Committee: about all of our work, the problems, hopes, difficulties, and the faith we placed in Al-Anon. At the end of the meeting, most of them were perplexed, and

---

[19] Leonella does not understand why the new National Secretary in Milano has never addressed the word to her, but the one message: Vincenza thanks her, and asks her to continue collaborating. Finally she invites Leonella *to be humble*, and to send *everything* by post to Milano. Vincenza was so far removed from reality that she didn't realize that you can't send an entire deposit of books *by mail*. At this point, Leonella insistently requests for, and is granted a meeting. The contents of that meeting, you can read in this paragraph.

one of them went as far as to say that 'everyone should have asked my forgiveness'.

Encouraged by an atmosphere that seemed less cold, I allowed myself to ask why they were insisting on the destruction of my own work and those of others, built over a decade; by eliminating the Roma Literature Committee, and to redo another one in Milano, where at the time there wasn't anyone who was able to translate from English. Vincenza's answer was:

"We can't tell you."

Despite the intervention of the World Headquarters in New York, and after I had clarified everything about our work, the decision to move the Literature Committee from Roma to Milano, and to remove me from all my duties, did not change.

One day of March 1983, a few Al-Anon arrived from Milano to Via del Teatro Valle 27, with a pickup truck. We welcomed them as friends and prepared lunch for everyone in a room of the Church.

As expected, we delivered everything: all the books and brochures of the deposit, the accounting books (as evidence of goodwill and proper administration); we also gave the stationery, even the pencils. They loaded everything.

After a short greeting, we saw the truck moving away, down the street, and finally disappearing around the corner.

We went up again for a final check, and looked around us: the rooms where we had worked with so much dedication and love for Al-Anon, were now empty.

But even if everything had been taken away, they had not taken away our trust in the Association.

Leonella - Public Information: a booklet to the Index (1984).

In spite of everything that had happened, I continued to collaborate with the new National Center.

I thought what was important, is that people who still did not know of the existence of Al-Anon, who were still isolated, and suffering, could receive the support they needed.

It is to them that my mind has always been committed. For them I fight. For them I translate. For their sake, I will continue to work as long as I can.

But let's get back to the facts.

As always, in 1983, I receive a booklet for the Public Information compiled by the English National, Al-Anon Center.

It seems well done, and I immediately write to London to find out if there is a copyright. They answer, that they are happy to be useful, and that the translation is not subject to copyright.

As always, I contact the World Service in New York, asking for their approval to use the information.

The WSO, as a sign of support, gives notice of the discovery of this booklet in its Report: the one that is made available every two years, on the occasion of the World Conference.

But it seems as if everything coming from Roma must be burned. The booklet is nicknamed 'the booklet of Mao' and the National Center of Milano, trampling on the approval of London and of New York, gives an unfavorable rating for the publication.

And more: during an Assembly held in Rimini, I was publicly reprimanded by a Councilor of the National Center.

While waving with one hand the Mao's booklet, she blamed me aloud in front of everyone: How could I administrate the Literature Committee, by doing such things?

The printing of the Guide for Public Information at this point stops because the Al-Anon Roman Groups, being few, cannot meet the expenses.

We have to thank Marisa di Dolo. Marisa, together with the Venetian Groups, joined the initiative by unblocking the stalemate in which we found ourselves. The number of booklets ordered, allowed us to get a price that matched our capabilities.

The booklet was printed in 1984. The attention on the matter was so great, that I still remember the cost was two hundred and fifty lire a copy!

Literature: the dates of the first edition disappear. The first ten years of work simply erased.

From the official Literature translated by Leonella and by other Al-Anon members in the first decade, the dates of the first edition have disappeared. In this way, the memory is suddenly and maybe involuntarily is erased.

Leonella left us on 10 October 2014, but despite the sorrows she experienced with the Al-Anon, and despite the family troubles, she continued to translate for Al-Anon until her physical conditions allowed her to do so.

The habit of printing only the year of the last edition and not reporting the previous ones, on the pamphlets and books, means the negating of Al-Anon's early history and with it, the gratitude towards our pioneers. To publish the printing edition year, would be a substantial gesture of love and esteem towards the friends who preceded us, and would also be the best and most authentic way to remember and honor their memory.

Mario - Via dei Banchi Nuovi

He calls for us. He does not want to die. As always, he tried to commit suicide, hoping that someone in the world will become aware of his suffering. Someone who is able to help him. It's about seven o'clock in the evening when we arrive there.

Mario has injected into his veins boiling water, containing I do not remember what, and also air, which has fortunately gone out of the vein.

Thankfully he did not succeeded. Only got a bad burn being the end result. Doctor Virgilio Pau, a great friend of ours, who was immediately called for, managed to heal him in the space of a fortnight, with the aid of his herbs.

Chapter Eight

Leonella's Report on the official New York Meeting[20] and the friendly encounter with Lois.

Dad isn't there. He has to work.
Alessandro is not there. I do not know where he is.

After 1986, for her work my mother Leonella received official rec-ognition from the Italian General Service Office, based in Milano.
However, the first part of the Report she wrote about the New York Meeting of 20-23 September 1982 was never distributed to the Groups. Fortunately I have a copy of it. The second part of the Re-port was never in my possession. I hope that one day someone will bring the document back to light, to share it with everyone.
Thinking that many Al-Anon might like it, here is the first part.

---

[20] The Report (I and II part) was never sent to the Groups, nor was the reason for not doing so, ever explained. We now publish the first part.

SECOND INTERNATIONAL MEETING
OF THE WSO in NEW YORK

September 1982

*Back home, Leonella addressed the following letter to all
the Al-Anon Groups in Italy*

Dear friends,
*This is the first part of my report on the 2nd International Meeting
of the General Services, which took place in New York from 20-23
September 1982, to which I had the pleasure of being the Delegate
from Italy.*

*The first of these meetings took place in New Orleans on the 7th of
July, 1980. On the 45th Anniversary of the A.A. Foundation.*

*For those who are not aware, It's my pleasure to recall that this
meeting came, like many other decisions already taken in the past by
the WSO, as a response to a need felt worldwide by the Al-Anon
members. The theme of the conference this year was:*

SHARING EXPERIENCE,
STRENGTH AND HOPE WORLDWIDE

Purpose statement

[In the official report of N.Y. WSO we read:]
*"The purpose of this meeting is to share the experience of the Na-
tional Services around the world through their Delegates. The goal
is to try to encourage the growth of a solid structure of service, and
to maintain our unity in the world through Al-Anon Traditions.*

*The Meeting also represents the expression of the groups' global
consciousness. Finally, and this brings us to the primary purpose of
Al-Anon as a whole: which is to seek the best way to carry the mes-*

sage of recovery to the families and friends of alcoholics, while working in different cultures and with different languages."

From the above passage, it is clear that these meetings are meant to bring together representatives of the General Services[21] of all the countries where Al-Anon has a National Center, or intends to have one.

Often the Al-Anon members are worn down by the weight of their responsibilities. So the aim of the Meeting is to give them the possibility to get in touch with friends who are equally committed to the service nationwide. Allowing them to exchange experiences about the problems concerning the establishment of their own General Services.
For those who are new in Al-Anon, I'll tell you briefly what are the 'facilities'-or general services-that a National Center should promote: an Al-Anon letter- Literature-Public Information (as well as internal information)-Work in Institutions. Each service has to operate through a committee.

And now that we know what "GSM -General Service Meeting" means, come on, all together, to New York! Yes, because the first thing I have to say at this point is that I wanted to have with me all of my friends, all of you. So follow me... between the lines.

*

I left with Patricia, a British citizen and a friend of mine in Al-Anon. She was to attend as an observer. We happily arrived in New York, late in the evening, on Friday 17 September, with just enough time to unpack our suitcases and go to sleep.

---

[21] General or National

The day after, I called Mary Ann K., happy to let her know, that I had already arrived. She gave me an appointment for the afternoon. Mary Ann was in charge as 'International Secretary'.

She was in charge for contact with foreign countries, and it is to her that we were writing, when we had something to communicate. It has been really a pleasure to be greeted by someone so attractive and gentle.

That evening (the first day) we met her in the Hall of the Halloran House, we also met the Delegates from Japan, Switzerland, and Australia, and we had dinner together.

All Delegates had booked rooms in the same hotel, located in the center of Manhattan; where we also had a few meetings. The day after, on Sunday, other Delegates arrived.

We had to register, and were given a folder, or brochure, with all the documents of the Congress. For in the evening, the Agenda was foreseeing an informal Al-Anon meeting; with coffee and refreshments, which was open to the Delegates and to their guests. But it turned out to be a meeting where everyone was called to tell how he/she had arrived in Al-Anon, and what kind of changes this had brought to his/her life.

I thought they would call only the Delegates with whom an earlier agreement had been made. Instead, I realized that 'everyone' was supposed to give his/her witness when Sandra. F. -the first International Secretary with whom I came into contact with- invited me to the microphone. I did not lose heart and, according to Patricia, I outlined my experiences with Al-Anon very well. Whilst speaking, I felt welcomed with affection. That evening it became evident, that no matter where we came from we were all 'alike' in a very special way, just like it happens in our group meetings at home.

Monday morning, we all went to visit the WSO (World Service Office). The headquarters of the Office has an impressive main en-

trance on Park Avenue, which is one of the finest if not the most beautiful street in Manhattan.

With this first impression of luxury, it immediately contrasts with the modest furniture of the Office inside. It is clear that according to American habits, there is not even one wasted penny, in the narrow sense of the word. Because they only care about making services more efficient, communications faster, and the World Headquarter more effective.

The WSO today[22] has 19.000 groups in 90 countries around the world. I had the great pleasure to shake hands and embrace Al-Anon friends: intelligent, efficient, and qualified Secretaries. My group was led through the offices by Pamela, who I had met in Roma. At the time no one could imagine that one day she would work at the WSO and that I would go to New York! God's ways are truly mysterious.

Each secretary has his/her own office, and each room has a different character that reflects the soul of those who are working in it. In a few places there is an abundance of different kinds of plants, kept with great care; in others there are family photos or objects. Certainly, a few of them are memories left by visitors.

We can safely say that in Italy we would define those desks, shelves and anything else, as very modest. Luxury, if we want to use the word, is all in the machinery: some of them very sophisticated and modern; but they have to serve the Association. One thing that is common to all the secretaries with whom I stopped to talk to-and I particularly remember Mary Ann, Linda, Hildegarde, Margaret, Sandra-is the enthusiasm for the work they do. The fact is, working for Al-Anon is not just a job.

We went back to the hotel in time for the Opening Dinner, which took place in the Fountain Room. Lois, founder of Al-Anon, was

---

[22] September 1982

present with Henrietta S., who is her close collaborator since the early days of the Association. Henrietta S., also happened to be the first paid-employee of the first Al-Anon office in New York. They welcomed us with a short speech that I summarize here:

'The WSO had a very modest beginning; and at the international level there still was much to be done. A fact which soon became evident, considering the number of people present: only 36 persons representing 21 countries, while Al-Anon had already spread to 90 countries.'

Early in the afternoon, in the Hall of the Vanderbilt Halloran House, the Second Meeting[23] of the General Services officially started. After the opening speech, when Cay C. began the appeal; I believe that when each one of us answered ' here', it took shape inside, almost concretely, the sense of responsibility that we had towards our own country, and towards the Association; that had contributed so generously to allow this meeting to take place.

Argentina was missing due to the problematic conditions in their country. Spain also was missing: for like Argentina, they too would have liked to attend, but had no one who could speak English and was also familiar with the topic of 'structures'.

C. Cay, who brilliantly chaired all the meetings through all the sessions, was visibly moved. Her words made us feel how close she was to us. We also felt that between us and the leaders of the WSO, in addition to the absence of barriers, there was also a sense of unity. After the speech of Cay C., there was the presentation of the secretaries. Each of them was given five minutes to talk about his/her Committee and about the work that was taking place. Following the program, two hours were devoted to the many questions that the Delegates had. The WSO Secretaries answered, alternating each other according to the topic.

---

[23] The first Meeting took place the year before (1981)

Tuesday 21, in the morning, the Delegates shared 'Experience, Strength and Hope', and each of us read a speech of one page. The text had been approved in advance by the WSO. In the afternoon, we were divided into three working groups; each Group gathered around a table to deal with the following topic: "How to encourage members to contribute to the service and remain in the service." We participated in a Group involving delegates from Italy, Finland, Japan, Belgium, Germany, Norway, Switzerland. Henrietta S. participated in our Group as WSO Representative. At 15.45 pm, back to our seats, we spoke about the need to improve communication between the General Offices of our countries.

Wednesday 22, the morning began with an exchange of ideas on how and where to hold the next international meeting.
Each Working Group had appointed a Chief in charge of reading the summary report of the discussion held about the problems relevant to the service in Al-Anon. Then the Groups met again, and they treated another topic: 'Sales and distribution of Literature': the relevant statements were read the day after (Thursday).

In the same morning, a 'spiritual' meeting took place, in which the Japanese and the English Delegates gave their testimony of faith. The result being that the two interpretations of this concept being very different to each other.

The second 'International General Service Meeting' was over, but we had not finished our day of 'Tourism in Al-Anon.' In fact, for lunch we were taken right to the WSO, which we had already visited the first day. About sixty employees were working there. After lunch, on coach, we went to Lois's home. As planned, she was waiting for us.

To go to Lois' home by coach, starting from the Al-Anon WSO Headquarters, it took us about an hour, but it was an hour of pleasant driving, thanks to the beautiful places that we passed through. Shortly before arriving, we entered a forest of oak trees, which soon became   denser. After a while we arrived at a place where the driver could not go on. So we continued on foot.

Around us were all types of green and flowering shrubs, as we made our journey. At last we saw Lois' house. From the outside, it looks beautiful and picturesque. It's a wooden building with a ground floor and a first floor. Here and there, in this vast forest, there are other similar constructions.

We entered the living room, and found ourselves in a cozy, quiet and joyful atmosphere. Or, should I say, an atmosphere communicating a sense of calm and joy, making us feeling really welcome. On a table located in the bottom right, cups were arranged for tea and pastries. An Al-Anon woman and her young daughter served us almost immediately, with the affection of relatives who had not seen you for a too long time.

Moving to the left, I remember a sofa, two armchairs perhaps, and then a piano. At the center, were other small pieces of furniture and cabinets.
Pulling back to the entrance I could see a door on the left, leading to a bedroom, while on the right, close to the center was a narrow, short staircase leading to the first floor, where the study of Bill was located, as it had remained as before: His desk, his belongings, his glasses. All around a 'grey wooden shelf'. Was it done by Bill with his own hands? It could also be.

The tray is full of books and objects, coming from all over the world. Things of all kinds, mainly with no value, but given and received with love. For this reason they are kept with the utmost care, and put more or less in plain sight, I think, depending on the aesthetic sense of Lois. She is certainly giving to all those memories the same priceless value.
The 'grey wooden shelf' was sheltered by a curtain held with two small nails. Behind, since the tent is not closed but only juxtaposed,

you can see the 'home items', that clearly couldn't be placed somewhere else.

Many other things were moving me: like a corner furnished as a workroom, with all the wires put in good order, along with scissors, thimble, metro and so on. In short, Lois home was telling us a story, allowing us to understand it, and teaching us many things.

After a while, I surprised myself into thinking that I was visiting the wealthiest house in the world, because it would be hard to find another so full of testimonies of love: the love of those who gave them and of those who received them. Lois was able to provide the most suitable place for any object, and it is perhaps why, subconsciously, she had created such a pleasant and characteristic place.
I have not yet written about Lois, because I just wanted to end this by remembering her.
Lois was there to receive us graciously, with her figure so frail and strong-willed. Always kind, smiling. When her bright eyes looked at you, you had the perception she in turn, had already understood you. Affectionate with everyone, she willingly allowed us to photograph her, and cheerfully talked to everyone. What is difficult to express in words, was the impression she gave of herself: someone who was deeply and truly authentic. The respect that everyone (rightly) gives her, does not weigh on her. Although she has been in Al-Anon, for longer than anyone else, she remained a fair and honest friend, an 'Al-Anon' among other Al-Anon. When I hugged her, before leaving her with so much melancholy, in her eyes a smile was shining. And this is the way I shall always remember Lois.

That last half day in New York was filled with messages and teachings. I could see the things I believe in. I had the proof that the philosophy of Al-Anon can be put in place, and that it works in all parts of the world. For those who put it into practice in their lives are always gratified

This report shall be followed by a second part, specifically dedicated to the topics of the three days of the Meeting.

Leonella

[To write the second part of the Meeting, my mother wanted to wait for the Official Report of the WSO. She wanted to make sure that a complete and well detailed report was made. The correspondence shows that this second part was also written and sent to the National Center, but never sent to the Groups. Unfortunately, I never got copy of it.]

Chapter Nine

Fragments
"The moon turned its cold face..."

> *Dad is not there. He must work.*
> *Alessandro is not there. I do not know where he is.*

This night
In a sky of gray dust
The moon turned its cold face
Covered by ancient veils of clouds
And it looked at me
Then this remote boat
Dripping with white and shabby green
has sailed to other skies
All in the shadow forgetting [mc]

Dreaming dreaming
To dream is to go crazy
Not to dream means to die
How to dream without going crazy
How to live in reality without dying [u.a.]

Mario- Forty admissions to clinics.

From 1960 to 1992, Mario endured many hospitalizations in clinics and hospitals to detoxify from physical and mental states that were annihilating him. The cause always was alcohol abuse, often mixed with drugs.

To these trials must be added the many nocturnal calls and the suicide attempts, that took place over thirty years.
Someone may think that a missed suicide, since it was an 'attempt', is not a dangerous one, or at least it is a fake. It is not so. An attempted suicide, according to my experience, is put into action with all the devices needed for death. However one must keep in mind that the attempt to take one's life, is always a cry for help. For the fight against the instinct of self-preservation is great. For these reasons suicides do not always materialize. To take your own life is not easy.

Let's go back to the notorious admissions to the clinics. My Mother's despair, and also that of mine, was that practically all the clinics had
-and still have- a bar within the premises. A sign of lack of professionalism.

There is no control over the patients who choose to go to the bar. In so doing they are undermining the reasons behind the hospitalization itself. Sometimes, going to see Mario at the clinic, we could observe he had dilated and dazed pupils. In short, he was more intoxicated now, than when he first entered the clinic. I particularly remember the day when my Mother protested with the doctor for such a 'recovery'.

The doctor answered:
"My dear Lady, we can only keep him quiet."
"But my son is addicted, and you're drugging him."
To which the doctor replied:

"Madam! We cannot do anything else! "

I think he was one of the few honest doctors we met. He was the only one who clearly denounced the limits of his profession.

Despite the clinics detoxified him after admission, it was useless; because Mario went down to the bar to drink. In the end, my parents took the decision to satisfy his wishes, and paid a doctor to put the famous 'Antabuse' under his skin. Antabuse is a substance that is meant to prevent the alcoholic from drinking. For if the alcoholic drinks alcohol under this treatment, he experiences a violent reaction.

But if an alcoholic has decided to drink, there is nothing in the world that can stop him from so doing. Certainly not a coercive method, even if chosen by him. Mario tried this grafting-method three times.

The day following the grafting, he began to do trials, taking minimal doses of alcohol. Although the quantities were small, the first time he tried, he almost died as a result of the reaction. But stubbornly, once he recovered from the fear, he continued with unsanctioned "small trials" of his own. Of course afterward calling us for help, usually in desperation.

28 November 1992 - Nothing more to hope for - Nothing more to be expected.

By the time he was fifty years old, Mario had got rid of a host of psychologists he had deemed as incompetent (which was true, except for the last one, who met him too late). At the same time he had renounced the attempt to quit of alcohol via mechanical means (e.g. Antabuse).

On a positive note he had understood that the family was not guilty and, in any case, powerless over his alcoholic problem. He had left

A.A. because 'yes', he could *stop* drinking; but he couldn't stop taking psychotropic drugs. Which was causing him going back to alcohol. He had been abandoned by his friends. He had become an obese fifty year old man, who had disfigured his face thanks to the dishonesty and incompetence of two plastic surgeons. The first one had agreed to remake his nose which, being slightly curved, made his face more enjoyable. Once he got fat, his nose seemed too small, and his face appeared unbalanced. The second surgeon had made a cut under his nose to raise his lip, and the operation had left the scar.

He was depending on his father who had learned to love him as he was, but it was too late. In the morning when Mario got up, he faced until evening, an empty schedule: devoid of meaningful action. Having lost hope of getting a job, his life became aimless. His words: 'If I only could have a job' he often repeated to me in despair. But he was never able to fully face the world, just like when he was a child.

Mario called me a few days before November 28: *'I decided to kill myself, as Giancarla did. I already have everything. And I do not want to weigh on your life anymore'*.
He has been announcing his suicide for over thirty years: so at one point, you no longer know what to say or how to react. Is it true? Is it not true? And what do I have to do in response? Do I keep watching him for twenty-four hours? For forty-eight? Does it make sense given that, in the end, you will have to leave him alone?
I had to leave for Geneva, were my voluntary work for the Committee against Apartheid was taking me. I did not even tell my Mother about it. Was I selfish and wrong? Am I guilty?
Am I?

A phone call: "Come back"

During the last days of November, I'm at the United Nations in Geneva. I have been working as a volunteer for some years in the Committee for the fight against apartheid. Usually the Coordination of the Italian Committees, directs me to the Meetings involving European Movements. I represent my evangelical churches: the Union of Evangelical Baptist Churches in Italy (UCEBI) and the Federation of Evangelical Churches in Italy (FCEI).

When the call arrives, I am in a modest hotel that the Italian Movement can afford to pay for its delegates. The phone is ringing. I pick it up: ' ...Mario... Come'. It's all that I remember about that conversation.

I understand what is going on. I have to call the concierge and say I'm leaving. I have to ask him to call for a taxi and in the meantime to help me, by booking the plane. But the input does not correspond any output. I understand what is happening and what I should do, but the actions do not follow.
Words, thoughts and actions have simply merged into a single dimension. I get out of my room and bump into someone I had seen in the meeting rooms of the United Nations. I take him by the arm and say, 'Please help me. I have to leave, I have to go home immediately, but I cannot think anymore'. 'Mr. Someone' does not leave me until he throws me into the boarding area at the airport. I still think of him with great gratitude.

The Morgue (1992[24]).

When in Roma I go straight to my parents' home.
They tell me: 'Someone called the police... It was last night...They did not want to let us see him..'. I no longer remember

---

[24] After Mario's death I stopped attending Al-Anon. Over the years I have repeatedly sought a dialogue with Milano but I never got it. In 2015 I respond to a request from Al-Anon on the Web: they are looking for collaboration for translations. My collaboration as a text reviewer, was first accepted, is then dropped without explanation.

why, and which party had warned the police. There was an investigation.

He had spent the evening with Alfredo Cohen, the last friend standing. When Alfredo had left that evening, Mario had put the plan into effect with determination.

This time, the *attempt* succeeded.

I think but of one thing. Mario is at the Morgue, and I have to see him before that damned coffin closes forever. It was not easy for me to find the Morgue and to force the officers to let me see him.
They allowed relatives, before closing the coffin, only one hour in the morning: between 6.30am -7.30 am.

The reason is that if the relatives do not go, they do not have to reassemble the body. But there was one other difficulty.
As soon as I knew he was dead, I had an intestinal disorder that forced me to go to the bathroom continuously. In such a condition, I should have locked myself up at home. But seeing him was the only way to process reality. I could not admit that I was late. Still, I cannot accept it.

I had to pick up the dropped stitches and reverse the route to catch him in time.
I could not accept that he was dead, having suffered all his life. I could not accept that night, maybe, he had sought help but, having taken peels, may be he wasn't strong enough or enough clear minded to compose a telephone number and call for s.o.
I could not accept the fact that I had left his hand.
Everything in the Obituary seems unreal to me. I went out of there with the same feeling I had entered: I had to reach him. I thought and thought and thought about how I could do it.
In the end, I had an idea, only one. So no matter how wrong, or out of the line and inadvisable it may have been, I decided to follow it.

I would enter the art world and would have put his name next to mine. In this way, I would have brought him back to life.

I started taking pictures.

The project was and is difficult and, even today, I have not completed it, as I would have liked. However, I do not give up, and I scored one point. I displayed my photographs in 2000 to the National Gallery of Modern Art in Roma.

I signed it as 'Laura Mario'.

Then I left to the Gallery-as required by the internal regulation- my works, and on the rear- in agreement with the Curator Elena Di Majo- I left as a gift to the Gallery some of the most beautiful photos of Mario, including a magnificent fountain of St. Peter captured in black and white, signed only with his name[25].

A dish of lentils (Genesis 25; 27-28).

Alessandro is not there. He has never been there. I remember the anxiety with which I was waiting for him when at last he returned from abroad. I had asked him for a meeting: only me and him, and we had arranged to meet at the *Laghetto dell' Eur*. It was the year 1976.

If we were together, I thought maybe we can succeed in helping Mario and to lift some of that weight from Mom and Dad. But where was I to start, in telling him about ten years of problems and dramas? Admissions, detoxification, delusions, the A.A. and Al-Anon, the Antabuse, the suicide attempts. I was a river in motion, and even before I met him, the words were already engulfing in my mind.

'Thank God', I see his car arriving, approaching, stopping. But immediatly after I see Alessandro getting out of the car followed by Claudio, his eldest son who is five years old.

---

[25] September 2019: I'm planning an exhibition of Mario's remaining works.

They come towards me. Alessandro holds Claudio by the hand. They are smiling. 'So what's going on?' I have a stroke: I cannot talk about alcohol and suicides in the presence of a child.

That day, closing every communication with me in such a strategic way, Alessandro showed all his genius. Even when present in Roma, he continued to be absent for us, for me.

One day, I do not remember on which occasion, I stared at him and words I never before thought came out of my lips like an arrow, catching both of us by surprise: *"You are not the firstborn. You sold your birthright to me for a plate of lentils."*

I do not think he ever forgave me.

My shortcomings. Emotional detachment

Knowing I was powerless over alcohol, I should'nt have considered as "a failure" my inability to help him. But I'm still thinking about it.

The second is no less severe, and concerns what is known in Al-Anon as, *emotional detachment.*

In Al-Anon, I learned that alcoholics have the right to suffer and that family members must get out of the way, and stop putting themselves between the alcoholic and the alcohol. Only in this way can the alcoholic realize that his problem is not his family (who are trying to help) but precisely the *alcohol.* This attitude presupposes the emotional detachment, which is required to help the sufferer. I knew the theory correctly.

For *emotional detachment* does not mean taking the alcoholic and throwing him down, even if family members would sometimes like to do so, albeit metaphorically. Emotional detachment means *taking back control of our own lives.* It means to deal with one's own problems, shortcomings, and perhaps even one's own spiritual health.

In fact, even if a person has good balance, it is impossible not to *lose* it sometimes when living with an *alcoholic* for years and years. Moreover, if we are the ones to get an alcoholic partner, in most cases it means that our balance was already compromised the moment we met him/her. Maybe it is because of loneliness, frustrations, a sense of worthlessness or something else. If a person takes an active alcoholic home, we may have doubts about what kind of problem he has, but no doubt he has one or more.

In the Association of Family Members and Friends of Alcoholics Anonymous, all the people who have been involved in alcoholism learn, in a non-violent way, to take back their lives.

Over the years, in Al-Anon, I learned several things that are still part of my behavioral heritage. Here is a small example: *put the most essential thing first*. When a day is too crowded with commitments, and I miss the breath, I stop and put them in a row: first the one, which cannot be postponed or delayed. And others follow in succession. I also learned to apologize. Now I find it even pleasant to do so. Apologizing heals relationships. Those who apologize are the first ones to enjoy the fruits of their action. Apologizing makes us stronger.

Resentment on the other hand, hurts those who feed them and not the people who caused them: therefore, they represent quite a senseless reaction. To eliminate them, I developed a technique. First of all, I imagine going out of my body, I put myself behind the person I currently hate, then I enter into his mind and try to understand what led him to the behavior that contributed to my resentment. If the exercise is well done, the irritation slowly decreases.

Mom, at least partially, succeeded in detaching emotionally from Mario. Having read, translated, and understood the sense of *emotional detachment*, she ended up staying at home to check my twin's behavior: to scold, cuddle, help or fight him. Combination of behaviors that are ordinarily present in a relationship with an alcoholic.

Albeit with difficulty and apprehension, she started going outside Roma with my Father in his long and tiring work-related journeys.

In Al-Anon we learned that alcoholism is a merry-go-round on which the alcoholic tries to get other people, drunk or sober: they are his audience, his company and often, even more importantly, his reason for drinking. Mom came down from that carousel.

On the other hand, in regard of detachment, I always failed. I continued as always, acting like a steamroller to give suggestions to my brother, to look for solutions for his life, and I did this even when I thought I had stopped doing it, and even when I really wanted to stop.

My behavior, over the years, gave my brother a level of suffering, which was destined to erupt badly. I was the one who had a job, the one who had not been rejected by the family, who could boast of being 'normal': reasonable, banal, bourgeois, and respectable. Which is easy to do when all the pieces are in place; or we make them seem so.

One day, furious, Mario threw me out of his home and tried to break off his relationship with me. Strange, that he hadn't tried it before. Odd, that he didn't try it again later. Family members often become an unsustainable moral standard for the alcoholic to live up to. For when they obsess over the alcoholic with constant suggestions on how to succeed in life, they in practice, also induce extreme gestures, which can disrupt his personality.

That day I went home and thought about the fact that it was time for me to stop with my teacher-suggestions: *"Do this and do that and do this."* And that I had to leave him alone. He died before I learned this lesson. Even after his death, I didn't improve.

I thought then, and I am still convinced, that if everyone had stopped suffering on his behalf, he would disappear from the plot of the Universe. It would have been like he never existed.

To prevent it, I chained our sufferings and hid them where no one shall be able to find them anymore; to rob them from me and divide us.

I too would be willing to melt his memory in the acid of time.
I would do it: if in so doing I could have the guarantee to dissolve
in the distant past, even his desperation.
I shall never let go my pain. Because I cannot heal his pain.

Mario's Agenda is empty

When I found myself wandering through the empty rooms of the small apartment in which Mario had lived, it was impossible for me to separate myself from the objects he had used or in someways cared for daily. Form the papyrus and the plants on the windowsill, which he loved so much, I found a beautiful garden in Anguillara; thanks to my friend Cristina, who still takes care of it.

I gave some of his shirts to a girl, whilst keeping for myself the box of his needles, threads, and shirt buttons. I also held on to his Agenda. I tried to find in it, notes about his life, but I only found a memo of no significance: "Given the water to the fish; go shopping; went to the metal head."

I couldn't understand why he had written such unimportant things.
Twenty-six years later, I realized that there was something impor-tant, in those notes, and it was the 'unspoken', the 'non-written'. I un-derstood it because, in a certain day, I surprised myself by doing the same thing.

I was looking at my diary. Nothing was noted in the last few days, and the blank pages reminded me of a feeling of unsustainable emptiness. The absence of life. Then I took a pen and scribbled what I could. However insignificant the notes, the ink lent a subtle form, and suddenly the Agenda was no longer empty, and I was no longer a ghost: I did exist. And I wrote, like he did: 'Cleaned home; went to the metal-worker; went shopping.'

I am lucky, for very rarely are my days empty. To him, this fortune was denied.

Chapter Ten
In Leonella's Death

Dad is no more with us.
Alessandro is not there. I do not know where he is.

In Leonella's Death - Considerations.

Leonella died on 11 October 2014. At the time, someone told and wrote confused words about her.

I'm referring to a particulat text in which, among expressions of esteem, like restless shadows, there were words that once again alluded but didn't say: words that hardly stand out from the others, words that *justify her behavior.*

The author of that text, largely spreaded, subtly induced the reader to entertain the idea of possible faults on her side. Without specifying, once again, which ones.

In that text in memory, the events so far narrated were summaryzed in a few sentences, and the writer took care to apologize for Leonella's *past behavior*:

> '[...] *perhaps, not knowing the Service Concepts,*
> *she was a victim of personalism.*'

In so doing the writer, whilst granting some justification to Leonella, clearly posited the notion that Leonella '*really was guilty of personalisms*'.

I think I'm right if I say that no one should be accused, doesn't matter about what and why, in the moment he/she is most defenseless. The moment he can no longer answer.

Moreover, we should always give the Deads the honor of the truth. About *truth*, Steps IX and X are clear.

IX - We made direct amends to these people whenever possible, except in cases where this could have damaged them or others.
X - We continued to do our personal inventory, and when we were wrong, we admitted it without hesitation.

In the same Text, the writer quote Tradition XII[26].
The writer asks the readers for forgiveness because, he explains, *putting the principles above people*, means not to praize people. And goes on asserting: *"For once, however, we would like to reconcile principles with people, because we dedicate this testimony to a person who has played a fundamental role in the affirmation of those same principles that have favored our recovery and our awakening"*.

XII Tradition and Service Concepts.

I think it is the right moment to point out something about XIIth Tradition.
In the XIIth Tradition, the concept that   *we must always remember to place principles above people,* is strictly bound *to a particular way of breaking anonymity.*
To thank someone for the service rendered does not represent a break in the anonymity. One which must be referred exclusively to the relations of the members outside Al-Anon, and in particular, contacts with the media: press, radio, television etc.

---

[26] XII Tradizione: *The policy of our public relations is based on attraction rather than propaganda. We must always maintain our personal anonymity towards the press, radio, television, and cinema. We must especially respect the anonymity of all members of A.A. Anonymity is the spiritual basis of all our traditions, and we must always remember to place principles above people.*

The XIIth Tradition arose during the first period of Al-Anon life span: when many got *carried away* with the excitement of easy notoriety, due to the sudden interest from the media, upon discovering *a disease called alcoholism*. Moreover, the reputation of one person involves, inevitably the privacy and anonymity of others.

Personalism, in the Al-Anon lexicon, as far as the XIIth Tradition is concerned, meant and means breaking the anonymity for personal purposes. And none of this can be faulted with Leonella.

In the given interpretation of the XII Tradition, there was also a second error. In the text, the author *justify* Leonella because, perhaps by not knowing the Service Concepts, she was a '*victim of personalisms*'. But the Service Concepts[27] had already been read and translated by Leonella in 1983 and, moreover, they exclusively concern *the management of the Groups* and not the personal behaviors (see Appendix).

I would also like to underline the point that *acknowledgments should never be mixed with apologies.* And also that a smile, a word of gratitude for the service rendered, can warm the hearts of those who come to Al-Anon much more than thousands of fires. A thanks, a smile, a word of gratitude for the service rendered, can help people repair their emotional pains, and even help heal the deeply felts hurts of life.

I would like to close with a thought of Leonella, taken from her New York Meeting Report:

"[...] *I could see the things I believe in. I had the proof that the Al-Anon philosophy can be implemented, and that it works in all parts*

---

[27] See Leonella's Letter to the WSO, dated 30 April 1983 (Appendix).

of the world, and that those who put it into practice in their lives are always gratified."

In these words, I find myself.

Mario- 1964
Il suo sguardo triste sembra annunciare la tempest
della sua vita
His sad look seems to announce the storm
of his life

Appendix

Who's Who [28]

For the sake of anonymity, all Al-Anon and A.A members are only referred to by their first name, and followed-when necessary for identification-by their 'arrival number', or by the name of their particular Group or location. Therefore, we say Marisa di Dolo, Robertino I of A.A., Leonella of Roma, Gina of Milano, Bruno II of via Lupatelliand so on. Despite this, several names are fake.

Abi (Al-Anon) and Vauro (Alcoholics Anonymous)
Abi was a great partner for her husband, who was suffering from alcoholism. Vauro, who unfortunately passed away many years ago; also received total and constant support from her. Regarding the facts we wrote about, the judgment of the moral character of their actions: It belongs only to that entity which we call Higher Power.

Enrica
She worked tirelessly as Treasurer for the Literature Committee, whilst taking on the tedious task of sending brochures and books.

Gina di Milano
To Gina we owe the first translation of ODAT. Gina, with great dedication, never stopped translating for Al-Anon and as a member of the Literature Committee, she gave Leonella courage, strength, hope and friendship. Without her help, we couldn't have reached the goals we eventually did.

---

[28] In the text, as a sign of gratitude, we also point out the names of a few A.A. and Al-Anon members who have no role in this telling, but closely participated in its operation.

Laura

She is the daughter of Leonella and has been a part of the history of the Association since 1976. She is the author of the legal constitution of Al-Anon in Italy and was the first Coordinating Secretary. Laura started the first *teen* Group (young people under eighteen) and the first ACA Group (Adult Children of Alcoholics) in Italy.

Leonella

She has been an integral part of the history of A.A in Italy, since 1974 -at the time located in Via Napoli 58 in Roma. The first Al-Anon Group was established only two years later, again in Via Napoli. This book is dedicated to her memory.

Leonella founded the first A.A. and the first Al-Anon Literature Committee. For this reason, she focuses her memories through the vicissitudes of those Committees. Leonella, Maria Grazia, and Gina of Milano were the translators of the Literature, printed during the course of the first decade (1974-1983). Leonella continued her work in translating materials for Al-Anon, almost until her death (2014).

Leonella was the first Italian delegate to the Al-Anon World Services Conference in New York.

She translated part of the Al-Anon Service Manual dedicated to the Al-Anon structure; and along with Marisa of Dolo and Gina of Milano, fought for the spreading of the so-called 'structure', as recommended by the World Service Office in New York.

Mara I – Alcoholics Anonymous

In 1978 she was the youngest recovered alcoholic of the A.A. Group of Via Napoli.

She was eighteen at the time. Mara has signed these Memories as a witness to many of the facts here told. Despite having had a dramatic life, Mara was recently celebrating the fortieth year of her sobriety.

Maria Grazia I (Al-Anon) - wife of Italo (Alcoholics Anonymous)

She worked as a translator for the Al-Anon Literature Committee.

She collaborated in the reconstruction of the very first historical memories, and in 1990 she delivered them personally to Al-Anon General Service in Milano. However the representatives in *Milano* never forwarded them to the Groups.

Marisa di Dolo

Over the years, Marisa I of Dolo proved herself to be a tireless contributor to Al-Anon. For many years she dedicated herself to the growth of Al-Anon in Italy. She was also an irreplaceable friend for Leonella. Together, they fought and won many Al-Anon battles.

Vincenza

National Secretary in 1982/83.

Mario – Alcoholics Anonymous

Son of Leonella and Laura's twin.

Playwright and costume-designer. Brilliant artist. Who started drinking at the age of twelve: it began as a fun experiment. At seventeen, he was drug addicted and an alcoholic.

Committed suicide in 1992, after an ordeal that lasted almost forty years.

Mary Ann K. (M.A.K.)

She was responsible for contacts with Italy. An intelligent and sensitive person, she was a great friend of Leonella and all the Al-Anon members of the first Literature Committee. Many still retain a loving memory of her.

The Churches – Monsignor Silvestrelli and the Baptist pastor, Piero Suman

The Churches, which are often forgotten, are the longstanding and silent protagonists of the story of A.A. and Al-Anon.

We recall, in particular, the role of Monsignor Silvestrelli. At the very beginning, he powerfully sustained A.A. and Al-Anon, putting at their disposal the great location of via Lupatelli.

We also remember the two churches that gave hospitality to alcoholics and their family members, being content with symbolic remunerations to support the cause- as they still do today. The Churches in question were: the Episcopal Church of Saint Paul, located within the Walls of Via Napoli 58, and the Baptist Evangelical Church in Via del Teatro Valle 27. The last one, in addition to hosting of the Groups, also made available to Al-Anon a large room, for the storage of the Literature.

Pietro – Alcoholics Anonymous
He was one of the first sober alcoholics and was Mario's first contact. He possessed a strong charisma. He helped several alcoholics along the road of recovery.

Robertino of Via Napoli - Alcoholics Anonymous
He is one of the younger recovered alcoholics. Although profound dramas have crossed his life, Robertino (so affectionately as he is still called today) is sober. Convinced of the fundamental role of the family members, he created a Group that holds many open meetings.

Wendi
Being the wife of an alcoholic, she was both A.A. and Al-Anon. In 1974 she founded the first Al-Anon Group in Italy.

The Steps-The Traditions
The Concepts of Service

The Twelve Steps and the Twelve Traditions are a guide to personal growth and group unity. The Twelve Concepts are a guide to the Service. They demonstrate how the works related to the Twelfth Step can be carried out on a large scale; and how the members of the World Service Office can relate to each other and with the groups, through the World Service Conference. The main goal is to spread the message of Al-Anon all over the world.

A.A. has a parallel association, the gathering family members of the alcoholics, called Al-Anon. A.A. had its beginnings in 1935. Its Steps, Traditions, and Concepts were first adopted by Al-Anon, with all but a few modifications. As of today, hundreds of Associations have borrowed both A.A. and Al-Anon Literature for their specific programs.

At meetings, Al-Anon members share their personal experiences as well as what they have learned from practicing the Al-Anon Steps.

We have chosen to let our readers know the original Al-Anon Steps, Traditions and Concepts. This material is also being published on the web. They have been a tool for the spiritual growth of millions of people suffering from the consequences of the alcohol, and alcohol related illness.

The Twelve Steps, Traditions and Concepts of Service of A.A can be considered a virtual, 'World Heritage Site' for healing. As hundreds of groups have used them as the basis of their recovery programs.

Al-Anon Twelve Steps, Al-Anon Twelve Traditions and Al-Anon Twelve Concepts of Service are available on the web.

A.A. and Al-Anon Monthly News - n.1

Roma 31.3.1980

It is reported, for those who were not yet aware, that recently the FISPA (Italian Silvestrelli Foundation on Alcoholism) was established. The Foundation, the first of its kind in Italy, which aims to give life to an institution whose purpose is the study, prevention and treatment of alcoholism.

***

In recent times A.A. has often been a guest at Radio and television shows. The last time it was hosted by Grand' Italia, a program directed by M. Costanzo. The results were positive, so much so that our few volunteers had to endure busy telephone-answering shifts.

For those interested and had the time and willingness to collaborate on the telephone shifts, they could contact Pia (Tel... - 9.00 am-1.00 pm); to provide their name, telephone number, and the days and hours in which they could be available.

***

The 'Press Committee' is finalizing two translations. One concerns the 'Twelve Traditions'; the other is an Al-Anon publication, whose title is 'The Dilemma of the Alcoholic Marriage'.

***

From Gabriella of the A.A. Group of Milano, we learned that two other Groups have arisen: one in Parma and the other in Sondrio. Bravo to everyone!

***

15/16 March: two A.A. (Carlo, Mara) and one Al-Anon (Laura) were hosted in Pesaro by the CIM. With the support of the Municipality. CIM promoted the establishment of both an A.A. and an Al-Anon Group. For A.A. there is already a manager, and we count a lot on him. There is also a cashier: her name is Daniela, and she is an Al-Anon.

***

On 25.3.80 a new AA and Al-Anon branch in Roma was inaugurated. The address is as follows: Viale... - 00167 Roma. Meeting days: Tuesday, Thursday and Saturday starting at 7.30 pm.

Special thanks to Carlo for finding the office.

*****

On 28 March 1980, at the headquarters in Via Napoli 58, the third anniversary of the Foundation of Al-Anon was celebrated in Italy. Special thanks to Abi, the secretary of the Al-Anon Group in Via Napoli, who has taken upon herself the task of organization.

*****

The A.A. of Genova is sponsoring the new Torino Group. Good for everyone! We are waiting for other positive news.

*****

Our friends from Naples are working to find an office in that city. As soon as they find one, we will inform you through this 'Newsletter'.

*****

Welcome back to Franco, from Modena. Franco, around five years ago, had given life to the new A.A. Now he has put his phone number at the disposal of the service for A.A. Here are the days and hours of the meeting: Tel.059 /... - Tuesday to Friday from 19 to 21.

*****

A special greeting to Adriana di Bari (Al-Anon) who, in her city has promoted the formation of both an A.A. and an Al-Anon Group. However, the launch of these groups in Bari, seems to be particularly tricky. Let's tell Adriana not to be discouraged! She is not alone. That Group has the support and sympathy of all the A.A. and the Al-Anon of Italy.

*****

Please note that two A.A. Groups were set in Bergamo and Brescia. Two others are being set up in Chiavari and Savona.

*****

On 29 and 30 March of this year, Anna, Antonella and Mauro (A.A.) stayed in Ascoli Piceno, where they carried out promotional activities.

*****

Recently A.A. was officially presented at the following conferences:

28/29 February- Viareggio, FirstNational Volunteer and Public Power Conference (Laura).

24 March – Roma, 'Drugs and Alcoholism' Conference at the Nazarene College. Attending: Prof. F. Silvestrini, Dr. C. Valenzi, Prof. G. Bonfiglio, Mrs. I. Bonfiglio. (John).

24 March –Albano, Conference on the topic 'Prevention of alcoholism', which took place at the Prof. Garrone Institute (Carlo).

***

NB: Whoever would like to give us news to be published, must only give notice to the following address: A.A. - National Headquarters- Villa Bonelli- Via Lupatelli 62- Building E int.2 / 4 -00 149 Roma (tel. 06/5280476). And we will take it from there.

4 October 1980
Al-Anon – Incorporation Deed and Statute
An Extract

Coordinating Secretary Laura... Leonella (Arbiter)... [Laura worked to have members included in the Board of Directors, selected from all over Italy]. In the *Incorporation Deed* and in the *Statute*, we read:

"[...] Up to local groups will be constituted in a number no less than ten, the functions of the General Assembly will be carried out by the Assembly of the Associates... To the new established Board of Directors is given mandate [...] to convene the first Assembly for the approval of regulations; and for conducting the activities of the association and of the Groups. [...] Organization: Al-Anon is divided into Groups. They are operating in all part of Italy [...]. **Each Group appoints [...] the Secretary, who cannot act as treasurer** [29] [...].

[...]The Group approves the annual report prepared by the Treasurer [...] The Secretary will attend the General Assembly [...] The General Assembly is made up of the Secretaries of the Groups and those who hold positions within the National Center [...] The Group shall keep the necessary money for its own expenses. The Group will invest the surplus as follows: 60% into the National Center; 30% into General Services in America, and 10% into the local Inter group [...]. All those who assume positions of responsibility with respect to third parties are required to renounce their anonymity [...]. Regarding regional Inter-groups: These Groups may appoint a Delegate [or Regional/District Representative, RD], who may be a different figure from the Group Representatives [RG], who represents the Group within the Regional/District Intergroup [...] which coordinates and develops the activities in the region.

---

[29] Abi signed the Statute but continued to perform both tasks until 1981, when she became National Secretary.

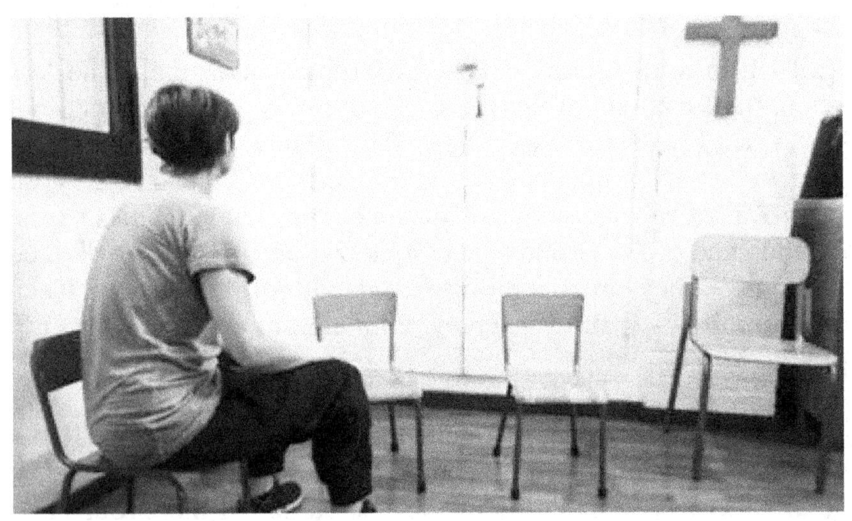

1976- The first Al-Anon are forced to sit in chairs made for kindergarten children.

Correspondence[30] – Minutes-Meetings
[1980-2014 Extracts]

1980 – Al-Anon first pamphlets.
Al-Anon participates in an 'A.A. Congress' which results, for the first time, of its own five Al-Anon pamphlets. Printing costs were anticipated by A.A., which now has 24 Groups, and is able to lend the money to Al-Anon.
[V. 1981, July 1982].

23 February 1981- Appointment of the first Literature Committee.
Beyond the request made by Leonella, who was already the Coordinator for the A.A. and Al-Anon Literature., the National Center meets (Gianni, Enrica, Abi, Mara, Rossana, Laura- Leonella guest).
They appoint the first Al-Anon and Alateen Literature Committee (Abi, who is part of the Committee, approves the decision). Members with technical skills are Enrica (Treasurer); Laura (Text Editor); Leonella (Coordinator and Translator). Members appointed for their seniority are Abi, Mara I, Gianni, Fiorella.

20 March 1981 -The WSO writes to Gina of Milano about Sandy, about 'One Day at a Time' and about the first sex booklets and the requested *copyrights* to the WSO (copyright: the necessary approval of the translation and publication).

27 April 1981 - Literature stored in Via del Teatro Valle.
[See Leonella's letter, 22 July 1981, sent to all the Groups]. Literature is stored in via del Teatro Valle 27, in Roma, where both Abi and Enrica and Pina are able to provide help. Abi is present and approves.

---

[30] The original correspondence with New York is in English. To facilitate the demands of the reader, it has been translated into Italian..

1981 April-September- Summary of activities - From a note drawn up by Leonella.

   * Literature transfer to Via del Teatro Valle (Abi was present and approved). The Committee is planning to translate even the Alateen Literature. (Alateen: Children of alcoholics between 12 and 18).

   * Thanks to a loan of 500.000 lire by an Al-Anon, having already received 300 bookings from the Groups, we shall be able to print 'The Dilemma of the Alcoholic Marriage'.

   * The Church in via del Teatro Valle offered to Al-Anon a room free of charge, in which to store the Literature (Abi was present and approved).

   * Report by Leonella on the work carried out by the first Literature Committee was to be presented to the very first Al-Anon Assembly on October 81 (Abi was there and approved the Report).

   * Print and/or reprint of 12 Tips..., Attitudes to be taken..., A Guide..., Liberation..., You love...

   * Leonella translates *Al-Anon 12 Steps and the 12 Traditions*.

   * Leonella informs us that by the end of 1982 'One Day at a time in Al-Anon' will be ready.

18 October 1981- The extras who are attending the first Al-Anon Assembly boycott it, as well as the notation for the approval of the 'Al-Anon structure' in Italy.
All the translation-work done by Leonella and Laura during the last years are lost, and Al-Anon is disbanded.

1st November 1981 – First gathering of the Literature Committee in Roma, Via Lupatelli – The Minutes: Leonella and Laura again propose the topic of the Al-Anon structure in Italy.
Attending: Abi, Gianni, Enrica, Elsa, Laura, Leonella. According to the A.A. and Al-Anon Service Manual received by the WSO, Laura and Leonella again propose the topic of the Al-Anon structure in Italy, and the network that should be formed by the Group Representatives (GR) and the Regional/District Representatives (DR). Abi, as the new Coordinating Secretary in charge since 18 October, with no support for denying her consent, approves the proposal. One which

she, only just a month before, to the Assembly she chaired, and by the extras, had rejected.

So the Al-Anon net-structure composed by GR and DR is confirmed. However, Abi didn't implement it. The pamphlets *Emotional Detachment, Only for Today* and *This is Al-Anon* are about to be printed.

20 January 1982-Second Literature Committee.
Following the suggestion made by Abi, who is now in charge as National Coordinator; Leonella convenes a meeting in via del Teatro Valle, where a second, exclusively technical Committee is appointed. Its members are Enrica (treasurer), Gina of Milano (translator), Laura (reviser), Pina (collaborator for Al-Anon News), Patricia (English speaking, for correspondence from New York), Patrizia of Pesaro (translator).

20 February 1982-Leonella officially informs Abi about the establishment of the new Literature Committee.

24 March -The National Center unanimously approves Leonella as the Delegate to the General Service Meeting, to be held in New York.
Abi approves. Also attending are: Gianni, Lella, Enrica, Fiorella, Elsa and Maria.
It is established that Leonella and Patricia will face the expenses on their own.

The minutes of this meeting is missing, but the notes are taken from Leonella's letter: dated 9 April 1982 to WSO (v.); from the letter of Leonella to the Groups dated 22 July 1982 and from the note circulated in Milano on 26 November 1982 (see paragraph dated 13 April 1982).

9 April 1982- Leonella informs the WSO she was appointed as the Delegate for Italy at the World Meeting to be held in N.Y. on 20-23 September 1982.

Leonella writes: *'[...] on March 24 our National Council decided that in September I will be the Delegate to the General Service Meeting (GSM)... Laura had already prepared [for the Assembly of October 1981] a graph, with which to illustrate how our structure could be in the future. I will send it to you to know if it is correct..,'.*

1982 May-June -Abi meets only with Deputy Secretary, Gianni, and appoints a different Delegate to New York.

The call for the meeting was never notified to the other members of the National Council, neither did Abi draft a report about it. Abi, however, says she let New York, "unofficially" learn about the decision taken on that day by the National Center.

16 May 1982 - The correspondence between Leonella and the WSO is censored.

Abi goes on fighting against the Al-Anon structure in Italy. She also takes control of the correspondence between the Literature Committee and the WSO. The censorship permits only a part of the communications, and was always late. In the letter of May 16, we read:

"[...] Yesterday I had the first five months of ODAT from Gina of Milano [...] There have already been seven revisions, Gina is doing another one [...]And then we will eventually send you the first part of the book hoping that the three years spent on the translation will give an acceptable result. Therefore the copyright may arrive soon... As to the GSM[31], surely you have received the Form filled together with my photo... [about the correspondence:] The Secretary of A.A. [in via Lupatelli] puts on one side your letters for us and give them to Abi. The consequence being that the last time, I only received your letter a month after its arrival. Laura - Secretary Coordinator in 1981- at the time went to Via Lupatelli every evening after the Office, and she brought me the letters addressed to the 'Litera-

---

[31] GSM (General Service Meeting) is the Yearly Meeting held in New York by one or more Representatives for each National Center, coming from all over the world.

ture Section' the same day they arrived. Now she can't do it anymore because Abi wants to see all the messages before I read them, and I seldom get them in good time.

Furthermore, if you attach forms or other sheets, perhaps due to the fact they do not know English, I rarely receive them... There is yet to be a Committee made up of Coordinators and District Representatives [regions]. In effect, the Committee of the National Center [which should be formed by the Regional and/or District Representatives] is currently identified with the National Center itself [formed by the seven co-founding Al-Anon members]. In Italy, we have now about 45 Groups, and they are certainly enough to give life to a structure...
I will send you the guidelines that Laura has translated to be sent to all the Groups.

Unfortunately, the National Council [chaired by Abi] has decided that it is too early to let Groups have this material. [To bypass this new obstacle put by Abi] the Literature Committee has decided to put the Hand-book on the price-list of Lazio Intergroup Pamphlets, so at least those who are willing to read it, shall be able to request it to us. [Then Leonella asks for the following brochures, which are next in line to be translated: P-43, O-44, P-45, P, 24, P-29, P-32, P-36,...]."

8 June 1982 – The WSO writes to Maria (the Delegate nominated by Abi and Gianni in place of Leonella (see 1982 May-June).
WSO informs Maria about following points: appointments of the Delegates had to be received before January 15; they didn't receive any official communication regarding the appointment of a new Delegate. As it later turns out, only Leonella was appointed. If Maria, going to New York, shall be able to save money on the ticket; and the remaining sum is to be given to the WSO, and cannot be used by the Delegate to stay longer, as Maria requested.

8 June 1982 – The WSO writes to Leonella on the following topics: Guidelines, Maria, the nomination of Leonella as a Delegate.
"[...] Thanks to the news you sent us, we realize that you really are a pioneer of the Italian Groups that here [in N.Y.], who will be represented by you for the first time. We are happy that you have translated the Guidelines [Service Manual or Hand-Book]: they will give our members the required help and guidance. We look forward to receiving you as Delegate from Italy.

Yesterday I received a strange phone call from a certain Maria. She wanted to know how to extend her stay after the General Service Meeting... I don't know if we succeeded in helping her understand that there is no Delegation Registration Form with her name in our offices, nor have we ever heard about her election. [...] Do you know anything about her election? [...] We look forward to receiving the first three months of ODAT from you".

July 1982- The new A.A. Bulletin, which is being published for the first time at the request of Abi, is also sent to the Al-Anon Groups in Italy. It contains a Supplement named *N.1 – Here Al-Anon*, which shall be nicknamed *Yellow Sheets*.
Elio of A.A. has taken over from Laura, the direction of the old 'A.A. and Al-Anon News'. In fact, it was decided that A.A. and Al-Anon must have different and specific publications. In the first issue of the newborn A.A. Newsletter, Abi nevertheless manages to insert *Supplement n. 1- Here Al-Anon* shall gain notoriety for the nicknamed *Yellow Sheets:* as it was printed on yellow paper.

The Supplement states that Laura and Leonella have no assignments, and ends up saying *they must get out of Al-Anon.* From the letter addressed by Leonella to the WSO in November 1982, it is possible to understand that the Literature Committee is being dismantled by authority, without making any prior communications justifying such actions, neither to Leonella nor to others.

Since the Yellow Sheets are attached to the A.A. Newsletter, they were both sent to the Al-Anon and to the A.A. Groups in Italy.
We do not know if a copy has been kept in Milano's Archives.

19 July 1982-Maria Grazia of Italo -a translator working with the Literature Committee from the very beginning, and also member of the National Council - answers to the *Yellow Sheets*.
She sends a letter to Abi and to the Deputy Secretary of the National Center for subsequent forwarding to the Groups. Such forwarding never took place.
The other members of the Committee also wrote to the National Center to affirm that the content of the Yellow Sheets was out of order, but their messages ended up in an empty space.
Maria Grazia also wrote to the editors of the new Al-Anon Bulletin, but again her message was not given publicity. The same fate faced the answers written by Leonella on 22 July (*see following*). Elsa (Literature Committee) and finally Laura, on 23 July. The letters - addressed to all the Italian Groups- were never forwarded. The so called *Here Al-Anon (the Yellow Sheets)* was no longer published.

22 July 1982 -Leonella answers back to the Yellow Sheets.
Leonella sends her response to all the Al-Anon Groups in Italy, but the National Center never forwarded Leonella's response to the Groups. The summary of her message: *Abi claimed to censor communications between the Literature Committee and New York, and we allowed it, hoping for a peace that ultimately never came [...] The new National Center has not drawn up the History of the Al-Anon Groups in Italy[32], as Abi promised several times to New York. Therefore I drafted it in Italian and in English, but Abi did not approve it. (see 23 July 1982).*

---

[32]It is an important document, as it must be read at the World Meeting of 20-23 September 1982, to which Leonella is delegated.

The document also states that the second Literature Committee was established on 23 February 1981. On 20 January1981 (v.), more precisely, the second Literature Committee was established, upon the suggestion of the same Abi, on the same day news of the meeting is officially given to the newly appointed National Center and to Abi.

Leonella's letter confirms that in the first instance Abi had agreed about stocking the Literature in via del Teatro Valle. And that Abi later, personally asked to return the Literature to via Lupatelli, without giving reasons, but that the National Center-which was not convinced- had postponed this decision indefinitely.
Leonella, in the same paper, explains that the Income and the Expenses [which Abi would get in possession] must be managed by the Committee, which being responsible for the debts to the Printer, must also control the income that is meant to pay off those debts. She informs us she is willing to return her mandate into the hands of the Assembly.

Leonella again speaks of the severe breakdown in the communication between the Literature Committee and the WSO. The problem is that Abi first wants a copy of the letters directed from Leonella to New York. Moreover, she has diverted all the correspondence from New York addressed to Leonella, straight to via Lupatelli. During the period of six months, Leonella receives only two communications from N.Y. The WSO, not having received answers nor from the National Center [where nobody knows English]; tries to get in touch with Leonella through telephone or fax.

Leonella is more concerned as Abi undertook to write, and then send a short Italian History of Al-Anon, to New York, but doesn't show the willingness to do it. Leonella is worrying because this is the short history that-as a Delegate- she will have to explain to the rest of Al-Anon, in September, at the Annual Meeting in New York.

22 July 1982 - History of Al-Anon in Italy.
The History of Al-Anon in Italy is finally compiled by Leonella. It is short, according to the specifications of the World Services Office (WSO). It is the text to be read in September to the World Meeting.

23 July 1982 - Elsa, Councilor of the new National Center, answers to the Yellow Sheets. The text is not forwarded to the Groups.

23 July 1982 - Laura responds to the Yellow Sheets.
The text is not forwarded to the Groups.
Laura, in the Yellow Sheets, instead of being praised, is blamed for having given life to the first Al-Anon Intergroup in the Lazio Region (four Al-Anon Groups and one Alateen).

Laura announces that the Lazio Al-Anon Intergroup was established following the guidelines indicated by the WSO and points out that even in Milano, for some time now, there have been Inter-group meetings. Laura expresses the opinion that the structure should be created slowly from the base; she does not consider it feasible or wise to have it imposed from above.
The Intergroups are moreover, already provided for in the Statute: also signed by Abi. Who on 1 November 1981 once more gave it a favorable vote.

30 July 1982- Meeting of the Literature Committee.
O.d.G: The Yellow Sheets.
The members of the Literature Committee gather to talk about the situation resulting from the Yellow Sheets. Amongst the others who are attending are Leonella, Laura, Maria Grazia and Elsa: the last two have a part in the Literature Committee, as well in the National Council. They elaborate, point by point, the response to the Yellow Sheets.

3 August 1982- Abi urges the New York WSO not to engage with to Leonella, and on 24 of March 1982, informs that a certain Maria, was nominated as a Delegate to New York.

Reading the first lines of this document, we realize the intentions of Abi, who states that a General Services Office has never been formed in Italy, as the Statute speaks only of a *National Center composed of five members*. She affirms that the decisions[33] for all the Groups in Italy are to be taken by those five people. She urges the WSO in N.Y. to stop communicating with Leonella, and sends them the Yellow Sheets, adding that unfortunately she was forced to submit them to all   A.A. and Al-Anon Groups in Italy. She denies the truth reported on the Minutes, (*see 24 March 1982*), and gives an unclear response about the nomination of Maria.

20-23 September 1982-New York Meeting.

Leonella draws up in Italian, the speech that she will deliver in English, in New York. Italy will take part in the International Meeting for the first time. For the whole Report (first part) see *Chapter Seven*.

30 October 1982- Report of the Litterature Committee to the National Assembly held in via Collazia 2, Roma.

'... the book One Day at a Time in Al-Anon is next to be printed [...]; the book 'The 12 Steps and the 12 Traditions of A.A.', and the brochure 'A teacher finds help in Al-Anon' are still undergoing translation. The translation of 'How Al-Anon developed in 14 countries around the world' is ready.

30 October 1982 - General Report of Leonella on the work carried out between 01 November 1981-30 July 1982. New Literature Committee proposed by Abi [v. January 20, '82].

---

[33] Incorrect statement. Upon reading the *1980 Statute,* we realize that it already contains the guide-lines for the future Structure.

November 1982-Leonella to the WSO.
Leonella informs us that she has had no news from N.Y for a long time; and that the new National Center, directed by Abi bases the decision of dismantling the Literature Committee on the principle of rotation.

Then Leonella adds:
"We have translated the World Service Handbook and sent it to our National Center in Italy. Although it seems as if our National Center is not willing to propose it as a Guide... Thanks for informing us that a Coordinator with special assignments can remain in charge for a period longer than usual... I wrote and sent the first part of my Report to Milano[34], but to write the second part[35], I'm waiting for your Summary, as I intend to quote it...
What concerns me is all the time that is wasted on defending the Service in Al-Anon from a few disruptive members of Al-Anon. It is really meaningless. As you read, we asked them [Abi] to follow your suggestions and information [...]. As I have already said, if we really have to stop the Service we are doing, we are ready to do it; but we really think we are responsible to the Assembly. The decision made by the National Center, to send to all the Groups 'Here Al-Anon' ['the Yellow Sheets'], containing the chronicle of how they decided to eliminate a Committee without even warning the Committee itself, did not set a positive example nor communicate a positive message."

November 1982 – Leonella to WSO – Again asks opinion on the principle of rotation - *Leonella to the WSO: Explanatory Notes and Observations.*

---

[34] Leonella is here referring to the New York Meeting of 20-23 September 1982, in which she participated as a Delegate from Italy. The National Center did never send her Report to the Groups.

[35] Also the second part of the Report was sent to the National Center but, as it was for the first part, it was never circulated within the Groups. Should it still be in the Archives, it would be worth finally sending it to the respective parties.

Leonella once again supports the right-after so much work- to be at least informed about the following points.

- The reasons for such radical and punitive actions, as an unjustified transfer of the Literature Committee from Roma to Milano;

- The constitution of a new Literature Committee exercised by authority.

- The ban on her from partaking in any further assignment in Al-Anon, except for the 'permission' granted to her, to continue translating.

All this was in violation of the Statute of the decisions taken unanimously, and in accordance to the principles of the Second Tradition: 'For our group purpose there is but one authority— a loving God as He may express Himself in our group conscience. Our leaders are but trusted servants— they do not govern. [the WSO will answer November 22, 1982-v.].

10 November 1982 – The WSO responds to Abi's letter on the following topics: Yellow Sheets, Leonella as the Delegate to New York, structure.

"[...] Leonella's work has allowed excellent Italian translations of our Literature, and we have seen an expansion of translations in recent years. The deadline for the registration of our Delegates to GSM was January [...] We read the translation of your first Bulletin [The Yellow Sheets] sent to the Groups in Italy: it is sad you couldn't solve your differences of opinion without bringing them to the attention of the Groups. This type of conflict could shatter a structure that is still in its infancy, which could take years to rebuild it. Leonella sent us a new proposal for Al-Anon in Italy [...] It is the opinion of the International Coordination Committee that this is an excellent plan to follow."

19 Nov 1982 - Reflections on the lack of reasons for the dissolution of the Letter Committee.

[The Note is from an Al-Anon of Milano. There is no signature.]

22 Nov 1982- The WSO about structure and internal disputes- The WSO responds to the November note by Leonella.
They inform Abi, Leonella and the National Center that given their own experience, the problems can be best solved, only by the interested parties working together [and this is why the Headquarters of NY always tries not to intervene].
As the WSO writes: *'[...] the structure submitted to our attention is valid [...]'*.

26 Nov 1982, Milano - Notes on the Al-Anon   Literature Committee. The Yellow Sheets.
Written note by Leonella on the Meeting held in Milano on 26 November. Again she reiterates that all the decisions disputed in the Yellow Sheets have been taken with the personal approval of both Abi and the National Center.

10-12 December 1982, Milano-Second Al-Anon Assembly: Vincenza is the newly elected National Coordinator[36] -
The new Secretary of the National Center is Vincenza of Milano.
Leonella, as Coordinator of the Literature, delivers to the new Center a Report on the work carried out until then; a Financial report. The Report on the publications printed and stored, which she distributes among the Groups.

9 January 1983- Leonella writes to Vincenza a letter full of hope.
The new elections saw Vincenza of Milano as the new Al-Anon Coordinating Secretary in Italy. Having read the first and beautiful letter sent by Vincenza to the Groups (which is quoted in the documentation, but for which there is no copy). Leonella now opens her heart. *"Now -* she says to everyone *- the problems are over"*. And on 9 January 1983, she wrote to Vincenza, a letter reflecting her dedica-

---

[36] Till this moment the National Coordinators have been: Laura - Ott.1980/Sett. 1981; Abi - Ott.1981/ Sett. 1982; Vincenza: December 1982.

tion, her hopes and her love for Al-Anon. She also puts at the disposal of the new Center, her willingness to collaborate, and to provide the needed information where possible.

23 January 1983- Gina from Milano writes to N.Y: The first decision taken by the new National Center in Milano was to dissolve the Literature Committee of Roma - *(see also Gina's Letter to the WSO of 18 April 1983).*

'[...] I also think you already know that the Al-Anon National Center is now in Milano. Good: yesterday, at its first meeting, the new National Center decided to create a new Literature Committee based in Milano, dismantling the one in Roma'.

25 January 1983 - Vincenza to Leonella. A chilling answer.
Vincenza's response to Leonella's letter of 9 January is chilling. The new National Center, which first met on 23 January 1983, decided to move everything to Milano. The reason that: *"It is essential".*
In the letter Vincenza laconically enjoins Leonella *'to send everything to Milano'.* She concludes by saying: *'We are also keenly awaiting your Report about your trip to America*[37]*'.* And that is all.

25 January 1983 - Gina of Milano writes to New York.
Gina writes that she was invited to the first meeting of the new National Center in Milano (23 January). During the meeting she pointed out that the translations and revisions were done by qualified technicians who therefore couldn't be changed every year. She requested the suggestions of the WSO about the topic.

---

[37] Two things are to be deduced in Vincenza's letter. The first: that she has no idea of the size of the stock, therefore she completely ignores the reality of the work done by the Literature Committee in Roma. Second: it is clear that Abi did not send Leonella's N.Y. Report to Vincenza either. This is surprising, because the relations between Abi and Vincenza, as far as I know, have always been excellent.

7 February 1983- Gina of Milano to Leonella. The new National Center gives no explanation.

Gina informs Leonella that, during the last meeting on the 5th of February, in via Stratico in Milano, she still tried to have a dialogue on the topic of the Literature Committee and again tried to explain that it was a shame to dismantle a whole, well working Committee. But once again the National Center does not give any answers.

14 February 1983- Leonella to Vincenza- Letter with an attachment.

Leonella takes up the issue again, and once more points out that to shift, *by authority,* the Literature Committee from Roma to Milano is not understandable. Once more she repeats the point that no one gave even a single valid explanation on the matter. Moreover, the newly formed National Center is ignoring the suggestions coming from N.Y. Besides, the National Center would like to get hold of the *Committee Cash* on the spot.

Leonella specifies that to meet the credit demands that the Printer has accorded, one that relies on trust, the Committee must be able to manage the revenue for another four months. It wouldn't be correct to leave us with a debt to be paid in Roma, at the same time preventing us from receiving the money for the books already sold. Leonella encloses in the letter an explanatory note with supporting comments.

28 February 1983- Gina of Milano writes to the WSO informing them on the latest events and again asks for their suggestions.

In the letter Gina traces the work done by the old Literature Committee, and again she complains about the useless destruction of an enormous work done with so much love and declares that the two new recruits of the Literature Committee in Milano do not have the necessary knowledge of English to carry out the tasks.

Among those who were part of the old Literature Committee, only Gina was invited to join the meeting of the newly based Literature Committee, but does not feel willing to interact with people who are not able to translate from English. She closes the letter with three questions:

1. Why dissolve a well-functioning Committee like the one in Roma?
2. How will the new Literature Committee be able to proceed in the wake of what has been done in Roma, given that it does not have the people with the required technical skills?
3. What benefit can Al-Anon in Italy hope to receive from all this chaos?

She adds: *'[...] In the official report on the Meeting held in Milano on 23 January 1983, from the new National Center, we can read that the Literature Committee depends on the National Center. It is therefore taken for granted that the National Center can eliminate or create a new Committee without even informing the previous one...*
They say that Leonella lacks humility*... They invoke the principle of rotation... I hope to receive suggestions from you as quickly as possible'*.

3 March 1983- The WSO writes to the National Center of Milano. Topics: Al-Anon National Center- Translations- The Rotation principle.
For the first time, suggestions are addressed directly from the WSO to the National Center of Milano.
The WSO finally takes a position: first they underline that from Milano they must stop writing to New York in Italian. As it is not possible to overload their translators with the work of translating the daily correspondence arriving from all over the world. They then reaffirm that the translations of the official Literature must be carried out directly in English. As it is in all countries: for it help avoid incorrect translations. Finally, they state that Leonella has recently asked for the copyright (permission to publish) for four pamphlets: *A teacher finds help in Al-Anon, A carousel of fiction, Is Alateen for me?, Aims and Suggestions.* Then the WSO adds:

'[...] We will block the permission to publish until we know from you that there is a working group with some members who speak English. [Then, about the principle of rotation, invoked by Milano to disperse the Roma Literature Committee, they write:] It would be a big improvidence not to use the people who have already served in the group... I understand that you are interested in the principle of rotation, which is part of Al-Anon, but we must also balance this with a sense of continuity. Take, for example, our Council of Trustees. They are elected every three years. However, after this term, they can be re-elected for another three years. In this way, these members acquire knowledge and experience and have a stronger basis for making decisions. Moreover, our experience here teaches us that it is not wise to change a entire technical group every year. Please try to work with Leonella, until the time comes when other members shall have the necessary experience, which will allow her to pass on her duties to others in the Committee. In this way you shall serve Al-Anon in the best way [...] We had better to save our energies to reach those whose lives have been influenced by alcoholism'.

3 March 1983 – The WSO to Leonella. Topics: tasks, rotation, humility.

'[...] We are anxious about what is happening in your country... Dissolving the Literature Group now would definitely be a step backward [...] It would certainly not be in the best interest of Al-Anon [...] having the debt with the Printers and other responsibilities, you should - have the authority to fulfill orders [...] the members of the Literature Committee should stay for several years, inserting new technician from time to time [...] It would certainly be cause for confusion and an added expense to transfer the Office of General Services every year and every time that a General Secretary is elected [...] I believe that the word humility is related to truth, reality, and openness to teaching [...] When someone thinks he/she is humble, he/she has lost his/her humility ...'.

04 March 1983 - The WSO to Gina. What they usually do about the rotations. They send a copy of their response also to Leonella.

'[...] Here in the United States and Canada, we have always produced our Literature in the city of New York. It was in our highest interest to have the publications edited in the same place and translated by experienced members [...] The entire Committee is never changed at once. We know that continuity is essential.
If they had to change altogether, much experience would be lost [...] These members must know English as well [...] For our common interest we must build on the foundations laid for us by those who came before in the Service. We must use our experienced members to learn from them. It is not necessary to recreate something completely new at every new election: that would cause duplication of effort and loss of time [...] '.

15 March 1983 – The WSO writes to Gina of Milano: '[...] we think it would not be wise to waste the Literature Committee.'

'[...] Again the [WSO] International Coordination Committee has reviewed your letter, and we think that it would be very unwise for your National Center to disperse the entire Literature Committee without using their experience...'.

21 March 1983- The National Center gathers, and decides to go to Roma and load everything on a pickup truck.

No member of the first Literature Committee would ever enjoy an explanation for these actions. At the time, however, thanks to the corespondence with New York, the National Center of Milano- before
coming to Roma, to physically take away the Literature, it decided to
summon Leonella to Milano on the 27 March for final clarifications, paying for her costs[38], as they wrote on the minutes.

---

[38] ! While appreciating the courtesy of the gesture, Leonella will accept the invitation but not the reimbursement for her expenses.

27 March 1983- Minutes of the National Center meeting in Milano to which Leonella has been invited.

For the Literature Committee of Roma, there were Leonella, Maria Grazia of Roma and Gina of Milano.

Leonella exposes the whole situation, and someone even apologizes to her. But when she asks at last to know the real nature of the problem, they answer: "We cannot tell it to you".

Now the question is: *How is it possible to clarify things when you do not know which is the point?*

In the minutes we read: *'[...] After reevaluating the situation and reviewing it for the umpteenth time, no element was found to justify the change in the decisions already taken [...]'.*

To conclude: in the Minutes the National Center thanked everyone for the work done, but the decisions remained unchanged and always without explanation.

1st April 1983- Upon returning home, still shocked, Leonella writes to the Milano Arbiters on the Meeting of 27 March 1983. She feels lost because even an answer is denied to her.

During the meeting, they also clarified that Abi, since October 1981, had exercised a tight control, not only of the communications between Leonella and New York, but also between Leonella and the Groups; and between Leonella and the National Center of Milano.

Still upset by the meeting- during which she got the impression to be accused but hadn't the possibility to clarify the unknown accusation- she hastens to brief once more the Milano Arbiters, pointing out again:

'[...] I didn't expect my explanations could be of any surprise to you, because I had already explained everything in my letter to the Groups on 22 July 1982, which I enclose... Now I would like to explain to you, the Arbiters, how I was elected as the Delegate of the General Services in New York. What I am about to tell you is written in the Minutes Book of the National Committee of Roma on 24 March 1982.

At the meeting concerned, there were Abi, Gianni, Enrica, Elsa and Maria [i.e., the majority of the National Center of Roma]. The Council unanimously decided to Delegate me. Abi, who at first was opposing my nomination, however without being able to provide any good reason for her refusal, at the end of the meeting announced she would seek another person as a 'second' Delegate. I pointed out that the second Delegate should also have the necessary requisites and should have to be approved, like I was, by the National Council [...]. In response, shortly afterward, Abi spread the newspaper named 'N.1-Here Al-Anon'. She was writing, among other things, that I had attributed tasks to myself devoid of any significance: among others the task of 'Delegate to the General Service Meeting' and the task of 'Literature Coordinator', and she sent this 'special issue' also to New York [...] '.

Leonella explains here that to clarify any doubts with New York, she had requested and obtained a meeting for the signing of a declaration, one attesting that her appointment as a Delegate had occurred on 24 March 1983. At such a meeting only three Councilors were present, while Abi and Gianni, who had previously given their approval, didn't show up for the appointment.

As for the Yellow Sheets, from these documents we can understand that the evening when it was decided to publish them, only Abi and Gianni (Secretary and Vice Secretary) were present. As none of the other Councilors had received the call for that meeting.
Leonella continues her letter asking the Arbiters to act in getting the Book of Minutes, held by Abi in Roma. That was claiming all her statements. Leonella also asked the arbiters to ask Abi for the accounting books and for the correspondence of the previous two years [such documentation would have clarified many things, but nothing of the sort happened].

1st April 1983- Telegram by Leonella to Vincenza: Leonella is still looking for a solution to the transfer of the Literature from Roma to Milano.

'Dear Vincenza, I vainly tried to call for you. Please remember to put in the Report what I already clarified to the Council on March 27th. The Literature Committee in Roma does not oppose your decision but confirms that the transfer represents unnecessary expenditure and risk. A hug. Leonella'.

16 April 1983- Literature is transferred from Roma to Milano.
Despite the explanations given, the transfer of the Literature and of the Literature Committee takes place by authority and consequently leaves a painful wound in the Al-Anon Groups in Roma. Who never received an explanation about the decisions made in Milano at the time [and the stigmatization it caused, even after forty years, still remains].

Leonella writes: *'We prepared a little refreshment for the Friends coming from Milano, and we gave them everything: minutes, reports, letters. Even the chancellery, which was taken. As the pickup truck disappeared at the bottom of via del Teatro Valle, taking away the fruit of almost ten years of our work. We are all caught in a great vacuum of emptiness. Only the pain, of not having an explanation, remains. The pain of being accused without knowing the cause of accusation. The intervention of the WSO was worth nothing; the appeal to the Second Tradition was of no use; the Arbiters considered my explanations to be of no importance'.*

16 April 1983 - Via del Teatro Valle 27 Roma - Delivery Report.
Attending for Milano: Vincenza and Angela. For Roma: Leonella, Laura, Enrica, Maria Grazia II.
The stocks testify to the part 'translations with copyright', made at the time by the first Literature Committee.[39]

---

[39] The fax will become common in Italy only between 1985 and 1990. The use of the Internet will become commonplace at the turn of the 2000s.

N. 9 Brochures:
Freedom from Despair
Guide for the family of an alcoholic
Lois' Story
So you love an alcoholic
To the parents of an alcoholic
12 Steps and 12 Traditions
Understanding yourself and alcoholism
Attitudes to be taken and not to be taken
Why continue to suffer?
N. 3 Sheets
12 Family Tips
Just for today
Loving Detachment
No. 3 Books
One day at a time in Al-Anon   (ODAT)
The Dilemma of the Alcoholic Marriage'
Al-Anon Service Manual

18 April 1983- Gina of Milano, about the birth and development of the Literature Committee in Italy.

Gina retraces the stages of growth and work done by Leonella and the other members of the first Literature Committee.

She writes: *'[...] The National Center of Milano, at its very first meeting on 23 January 1983, decided to dissolve the Literature Committee in Roma. To which they immediately asked to send everything to Milano'. She also complains about the lack of explanations and complains about the fact the new National Center in Milano has never disclosed the suggestions received from N.Y., nor did they take it into any account [...].*

18 April 1983- Gina writes to the WSO. Letter sent in copy to Leonella and Vincenza.

Topics: transfer of the Literature from Roma to Milano; Leonella in Milano: how is it possible to 'clarify' things if you do not know which is the point? The new Committee in Milano is formed with the help of "translators" who did not know English.

'[...] Despite your letters to me, to Vincenza and Leonella, in Milano they didn't change the decision to dissolve the well-functioning Literature Committee of Roma. On 16 April 1983 four Al-Anon members went from Milano to Roma. They collected everything in a pickup truck [...] On 27 March 1983 our National Center in Milano held a meeting. Vincenza, the Councilors, the Arbiters, Leonella, Maria Grazia of Roma and myself are present. Leonella was allowed to provide information only at the end of the meeting. I can't recall any convincing answer either from Vincenza or from others [...].

After several hours of meeting, the decision that was taken, was the same as the National Center had taken at its first meeting on 23 January 1983, that is, to bring everything to Milano and to dissolve the Roma Literature Committee by authority.
Needless to say, that the new Literature Committee in Milano is formed by M. and L., who does not know English [...] '.

30 Aprile 1983- Leonella to the WSO– Someone apologized, but the decision to knock down the Literature Committee of Roma in one fell swoop remains unchanged. They told me: "There is a reason [...], but we cannot tell it to you".
'[...] I wrote to Vincenza telling her that [in Italy] they ought not to ignore the letters of Lazio and Veneto Intergroups, nor the suggestions of the WSO itself. The result of the meeting of March 27 is that they apologized to me, and one of them admitted 'they were making a great mistake'. However in the end, they decided to keep the point and when I asked which were the reasons to knock down the Literature Committee of Roma, Vincenza answered: 'There is a reason, but we cannot tell it to you [...]'.

I have translated 'The 12 Service Concepts', *and I 'm sending them to Gianna, but still I have difficulty with the translation of the following sentence, found at the start of page 38:*

'To publish in paperback (economic edition) would not be an answer, either: publishers tell us that paperback issues nearly always destroy the circulation of hardcover books'.

If you could give us some explanations, we should be very grateful. They asked me not to miss my collaboration, and I will, but I know it will be very challenging. We consigned all the Literature in our store (around 20 million lire) with no debt and over 1 million lire in credit. Which means we paid off 'One Day at a Time' in about three months. The mother of Maria Grazia has finished translating '12 and 12', and I will make the first revision; then Laura and Maria Grazia will review it again. Meanwhile I have translated 'Homeward Bound' and 'Three Views of Al-Anon', but I will not deliver anything until they have demonstrated that they can translate from English...[at this point Leonella asks WSO specifications on an unclear sentence of the '12 Service Concepts'. Then she continues:]

*I have already asked you for a copy of the Report of the GSM (General Service Meeting of 20-23 September 1982). **I'm waiting for it, to move forward with the second part of my report.** Please send it as soon as possible to my address. We hope that the National Center of Milano will not implement what they have promised, which would be to put into circulation a large quantity of photocopied pamphlets translated from French, without copyright, also including not 'officially approved Literature'. The Lazio Intergroup sent a letter to Vincenza, recommending not to put this resolution into practice. The same position is supported by the Veneto Intergroup [...] '.*

06 May 1983- WSO writes to Gina, and reiterates the importance of translating directly from English.
Then they add: *'[...] It is also important to have someone at the National Center to take responsibility for communicating with us in English, keeping us informed about the activities in your country [...]'.*

25 June 1983 - Gina answers to WSO about translations.
Gina informs she has completed the translations of *Al-Anon Goals*, *Adult Children of Alcoholics, Information for the Newcomer*. She informs that two translators reviewed the pamphlets and found them to be correct; therefore she requires the copyright. On behalf of Vincenza, she also asks for the copyright for some translations which were already in their hands.

13 July 1983 – The WSO to Vincenza.
The WSO thanks Vincenza for writing them in English and for giving them the news. *'[...] We appreciate you giving us the name of the four new translators. Right now we are about to receive back from C. [WSO staff for revision of translations] the pamphlets you sent us. We want you to know that 'Sponsorship', 'What it's All about' [...] require a little more time for their revision... we suggest that you don't print them out, so you won't find yourselves staggered with the authorization dates [...]'.*

13 August 1983- A message from Lois.
Lois received a copy of 'One Day at a Time' translated into Italian, and thanks warmly the Literature Committee in Rome.

23 August 1983- About the importance of translating from the *original.*
The WSO writes to Gina about the translation of *Why the Anonymity in Al-Anon*. She reiterates the importance of translating the documents from the original.
The WSO explains that it is clear that the translation, although written in excellent Italian, was not made from the original English, and that this is requiring more work for the revision. They reiterate that a translation can be faithful done only from the original language, without a double pass.

23 September 1983- Gina of Milano to Leonella.
Gina gives information on translations, again complaining the translation work made in Milano is resulting in oversights and mistakes. Gina also complains that the work of the translators no longer has the "triple revision", as it was customary in Roma.

04 October 1983- Gina to WSO.
The letter concerns the verification of the copyright-related to two translations not made by the Al-Anon Literature Committee.

29 January 1984 - Report.
Meeting of the new National Center in Padova: the Literature Committee remains unchanged. Now that Leonella is no longer there, nobody talks anymore about alternation of tasks and offices. Vincenza asks for the complete translation of the World Services Manual. However, not knowing English, she fears that something may be missed and she does not realize how much energy a translation of this kind requires. The Manual is full-bodied because it refers to the structure of Al-Anon in the United States of America, a reality far more complex than the Italian one.

February 1984 - Leonella writes to Vincenza on behalf of the Lazio Intergroup. Public Information.
The subject of the letter is the printing of the booklet for Public Information-which was opposed by both Abi in Roma and Vincenza in Milano. Leonella-by chance, finds a booklet from the British National Center for Public Information. She finds it could be of great help, she translates it, and then asks both London and N.Y, the permission to spread it and to use it as a reference. The National Center of Milano opposes the print of the booklet, and Abi adds fuel to the fire. In the letter, Leonella provides ample references to the fact that 'service indications' do not require copyright, and that in any case London, New York, the Veneto Intergroup, and the Lazio Intergroup approved the booklet. Finally, the World Services Manual explicitly

suggest the adoption of the proposed guidelines according to the needs of each structure.

05 February 1984 - Gina to Leonella about translations, Public Information guidelines, and the Meeting in Nervi.
Gina asks Leonella again for the translation of 'Purpose and Suggestions'.
She informs she is trying to make it clear that the Service Manual adopted in England, which is a relatively small country, certainly fits Italy better than the giant, American Manual.
Gina speaks about the Meeting held in Nervi, in which Leonella was left alone to address the subject of the structure to a hostile Assembly [Gina had to rush back home for family reasons].

14 October 2014 - The funeral eulogy of Al-Anon for Leonella (see Chapter IX).

Index

ALCOHOLISM and STIGMA

Chapter One

(Leonella) First contact with A.A.: a kind and caring person answers- Pietro (1973) - Notes on A.A. - Lois throws a shoe at her sober husband, and Al-Anon is born- Pietro dies, sober. The suicide of Giancarla and Elisa- A beautiful afternoon in May (1974) - Wendi- Alcoholism is a disease- (Leonella) When I translate, I seem to talk to my son- (Leonella) An embittered Wendi goes back to America: Abi wanted to kick her out of the Group.

Chapter Two

Grandfather Francesco- Alessandro: an obedient child- In Italy, they consider the psychologist as a misfortune reserved to madmen and eccentrics- Suddenly a glass in my hands.

Chapter Three

Alcoholism: a family disease. Al-Anon role- The first battles: the Program is also for the Al-Anon   members. The Group divides into two factions- The cash is to be defended- Your alcoholic is not sober: 'Out of Al-Anon!' – Al-Anon is strictly for the alcoholic's relatives: 'Friends cannot enter!'

(Leonella) In New York the meeting is moving. They hand me the copyright for 'One day at a time' (20/23 September 1982) - The National Center Al-Anon is transferred from Roma to Milano: 'Finally a hope' - Leonella- Milano, Assembly 10/12 December 1982: "They forbid me from reporting on the New York meeting. I am informed that my assignments are going to finish." - The meeting with the Arbiters turns into a monologue: no explanations; no answers. (January 1983) - Public Information: a booklet to the Index (1984).
(Laura) Literature: the dates of the first edition disappear. The first ten years of work are canceled.

Chapter Eight

Chapter Nine

Mario: Forty admissions to clinics- 28 November 1992- Nothing more to hope for- Nothing more to be expected- A phone call: "Come buck" - The morgue (1992)- A plate of lentils (Genesis 25; 27-28)- My failures. Emotional detachment- Mario's agenda is empty.

Chapter Ten

Appendix

Youcanprint
Printed in March 2020

www.ingramcontent.com/pod-product-compliance
Lightning Source LLC
La Vergne TN
LVHW010333200726
843507LV00010B/1481